G. J. (Gilbert Jasper) George

William Newby

Or, The Soldier's Return

G. J. (Gilbert Jasper) George
William Newby
Or, The Soldier's Return

ISBN/EAN: 9783337136536

Printed in Europe, USA, Canada, Australia, Japan

Cover: Foto ©ninafisch / pixelio.de

More available books at **www.hansebooks.com**

WILLIAM NEWBY

ALIAS "DAN BENTON," ALIAS "RICKETY DAN,"
ALIAS "CRAZY JACK,"

OR

THE SOLDIER'S RETURN

A TRUE AND WONDERFUL STORY OF
MISTAKEN IDENTITY

A NARRATIVE FULL OF STRANGE PARADOXES

OVER THIRTY YEARS A SOLDIER IN THE LATE WAR—THE LIVING HUSBAND OF HIS OWN
PENSIONED WIDOW—ACKNOWLEDGED AS HUSBAND AND FATHER BY HIS WIFE
AND CHILDREN, OF WHOM HE KNOWS NOTHING—A DEMENTED WAN-
DERER FROM ALMSHOUSE TO ALMSHOUSE, HE IS PICKED UP
NEAR HIS OWN BEAUTIFUL HOME—PROVEN TO
BE ALIVE BY COMRADES WHO SWORE
THEY BURIED HIM ON THE
FIELD OF BATTLE

BY

G. J. GEORGE

LIEUTENANT COMPANY D, 40TH ILLINOIS INFANTRY

CINCINNATI:
Press of C. J. Krehbiel & Co.
1893

CONTENTS.

CHAPTER.		PAGE.
	Introduction and Preface	iii.
I.	Early Life of William Newby	1
II.	Was William Newby Killed at Shiloh	13
III.	William Newby's Return	35
IV.	Marks of Identification	59
V.	Parallel Cases	67
VI.	Crazy Jack	79
VII.	Dan Benton	91
VIII.	Trial—The Prosecution	143
IX.	The Defense	171
X.	The Judge's Charge and the Verdict	233
XI.	Review of the Trial	243.
XII.	Conclusion	255
	Appendix	267

INTRODUCTION.

EARLY in 1861 William Newby enlisted in Company D, 40th Illinois Infantry, along with many of his old White County neighbors and friends. At Shiloh, on Sunday morning, April 6, 1862, when the rebels made their first grand charge upon the Union lines, the 40th met them in that deadly conflict, and in a few moments many fell. Many were killed and many wounded, and Newby, who was left on the field, was thought to be wounded fatally. The regiment retreated, and three days later his comrades thought they buried him with the rest. And this fact was so reported to the government. It now seems that they were mistaken, and that, instead, he was taken prisoner and carried away into the South to Belle Isle, thence to Andersonville, where, although he had lost his reason from the wound upon his head, he was kept in that pen, and known there as "Crazy Jack," his identification being complete. After being released he wandered over the world for twenty-nine years, finally coming to his own country, where he was discovered, captured, and brought home to his family, whom he did not know. Through the effects of kind treatment and familiar surroundings his reason was to some extent restored. In due time he applied for discharge from the service and for a pension. The case being an important one, the government put upon the claim its special detective and examiner, who, after getting Newby's disjointed statements, and finding he had been at Nashville, Tenn., induced the claimant to go down to Tennessee, where a fellow by the name of "Rickety Dan" Benton was known before the war. Benton had many points in common with the claimant, and the agent found many people there who were willing to swear that Newby and Benton were identical. He was then brought back from Nashville to Springfield, Ill., where he was jailed, indicted, and tried as a fraud. One trial is over, and another pending. One hundred and forty of his old neighbors swear he is Newby; thirty Tennesseeans swear that he is Benton; six men who were in Andersonville swear that he is "Crazy Jack"—Three in One.

We then undertake the task of reducing three to one, and that one to be William Newby, who served his country as a member of Company D, 40th Illinois Infantry, and to assist in restoring him to his family and to his rights as a brave soldier.

PREFACE.

SO greatly has the public mind been exercised over this strange matter, so famous has the history of this great trial become, so astonishing the verdict of the jury, and so eager is the public to get hold of the facts concerning this many-sided man, that I deem it my duty to satisfy public curiosity, and set forth the truth, which the world is sure to welcome.

I knew William Newby in my boyhood. Our fathers were pioneers, and worked many years on adjoining farms. We joined the same company when we went to the war. At the battle of Shiloh he was shot before my eyes, and I saw him writhing on the ground. Three days after, the men, his neighbors and mine, whom I detailed to bury the dead, reported that they buried Newby.

I believed him to be dead, so I reported to the government.

For thirty years I shared, in common with his family, his neighbors, comrades, and the world at large, the belief that the record was true. That convictions of such long standing should be called in question; that traditions, hoary with age, should be overthrown; that the records should be proven false, and that the grave should give up its dead, seems most strange.

The blunt, brutal fact is, however, that William Newby, the man who "kind o' quivered and fell over on his side" when the bullet struck him on the head at Shiloh, is to-day held prisoner by the government, for knocking at the door of the War Department, and asking for his discharge, and for compensation for past services and sufferings.

This I am forced to believe. So his old mother, his wife and his children believe. And such is the belief of thousands who have seen and heard the evidences of the poor old wanderer's return.

For the faith of these the public demands a reason.

That the case is full of mystery there is no question. In the narrative you have before you the wreck of a man who is recognized as being three different men once known in different states of the Union, all of whom disappeared from the sight and knowledge of men more than a quarter of a century ago.

A cloud of witnesses recognized him as William Newby, of the Company D, 40th Illinois Infantry, who was supposed to have been buried at Shiloh.

A crowd of witnesses from the South rise up and declare him to be one Dan Benton, a deformed and rickety boy, afterward a vagabond and "a mover-on on the face of the earth," who shambled up and down the "Granny White Pike" in Davidson County, Tennessee, many years ago.

Others know him as Crazy Jack, a wounded and demented prisoner in Andersonville, whom they had often dragged out of the slime and muddy water of that historic stream in 1864.

All these parties swear point blank to their man, and, making allowance for bias due to sympathy, prejudice, or politics, they swear to what they believe to be the truth.

The lives of the three characters, Crazy Jack, Rickety Dan, and William Newby, have become so mixed up in the minds of men, and so curiously merged into that of the being we call William Newby, that the truth concerning them may never be known.

In the narrative I propose to treat each of these characters separately, and hope to vindicate the claims of the old soldier who stands in the shadow-land where the light of reason sometimes stirs the dreams of the past, and helplessly he looks around and pathetically exclaims, "If I ain't Bill Newby, who in the hell am I?"

I hope, in these pages, to vindicate the judgment of the hundreds of old neighbors, old comrades, and old friends who now believe that Newby was not killed at Shiloh, but was stunned, disabled, and carried away a prisoner into the South.

I hope to vindicate the honor of the gray-haired wife, who believes that the man she now claims to be her husband to be the same whose love, cares and sorrows she shared so many years on the farm, now mortgaged to raise money for his defense.

To benefit the family of William Newby, financially, is, in part, the object of the sale of this book.

The bitter fight made by the Pension Department upon the old soldiers, and especially the tactics employed by the officers, have stirred up in the minds of many the questions—

PENSIONS? OR NO PENSIONS?

Will the government redeem its pledges to the old soldiers? or, Will it point them to the "two open doors—the poor house or the grave?"

While the sense of right and justice is deeply implanted in the hearts of the American people, it must be acknowledged that at this time there is great uncertainty and unrest in the minds of many as to the outcome of this matter, and the head of many an old soldier would rest easier upon his pillow if he knew it would be answered in the affirmative.

Men are prone to shirk the payment of old obligations. We often see a man who is willing to thrust off a father or a mother onto the cold charities of the world, not deeming the sacrifices of their early life to merit protection and care in their old age. It should not be a matter of wonder, therefore, that, after a third of a century, some men should grow weary of paying the debt due to those who defended the country in its time of need; those—

"Whose tottering steps and ancient scars
Are the living records of their country's wars."

Had this old relict of the war, this "last leaf," this solitary remnant of a mighty army, been permitted to die without applying for pension or discharge, he might have passed his days in solitude, surrounded by his wife and children, and ended in peace a life which for misfortune, mystery and misery has no parallel.

WILLIAM NEWBY AND WIFE.

WILLIAM NEWBY;

OR,

THE SOLDIER'S RETURN.

CHAPTER I.

THE EARLY LIFE OF WILLIAM NEWBY.

IN the interest of truth, and for the purpose of setting forth the facts in the early life of William Newby in their true order, I have, in this year of our Lord, 1893, gone to the archives, where all child-history is filed away, where all infant smiles and tears are recorded, where all youthful joys and sorrows, long forgotten by ourselves, are treasured, and, like the flowers from the coffins of our beloved dead, kept moist with memory's tears—to the mother.

Although weighed down by the cares and experiences of nearly a hundred years, and the fatigues of a recent journey in behalf of her boy (sad, too, for when she started to come home from the recent trial, she had said: "Tell them that I gave my boy to the government when they needed him, and now they ought to give him back to me"), the result of the trial, so unexpected to his prosecutors, so unaccountable to the community in general, and to his friends, brought deadly sorrow to her poor old heart. When I greeted her and spoke about her son, thinking that something was being done in behalf of her boy, she exclaimed: "Are you trying to do something for my Bill? If you are, I want to fling in something." Assuring her that I only wanted a few of the recollections of his early life, she returned a few coins to her pocket, and dropped with alacrity into the subject dearest to an old mother's heart—the hard days, the precious days, "when the children were little."

Running on, about as indicated, she mixed comparison with history in a manner which showed how closely she had compared the man with the boy. "I was born," she said, "in 1802. I had six sons and six daughters. William was my second boy, and he was born in Smith County, Tennessee, in May, 1826. We came to Illinois when he was six years old. We were on the road six weeks, and stopped a few miles from here in Wayne County. We raised three crops over in Wayne and then moved here. William was a good hand on the farm; for a boy, he was a powerful worker. When he was very young his daddy put him to feeding and taking care of the horses. That was a part of his occupation, for he delighted to harness and manage horses.

"In many things he has the same ways that he used to have. He works around horses the same way. He used to carry a pocket full of squirrel-skin strings to mend the gears with. It took two teams to keep William going when he worked on the farm. He would lead an extra horse to the field, and when the one that he was plowing got tired, he would work the other. He used to call me 'mammy' before he went to the war, and he speaks it in the same way now. He used to work so hard, and he would come to the house and say, 'mammy, I'm hungry,' and he would eat a whole pie. He does that same way now. William was a mighty venturesome child. He wasn't afraid of anything or anybody. I went off one time and told him not to fool with a wild horse that we had, and when I came home, bless you, he had caught that horse and had made him gentle, and had hauled a whole string of fence with him. He always wanted to conquer everything; wanted to break everything in, and that's his disposition now."

In these few rude touches we can see a boy that is hearty, hardy, trustworthy, fearless to a fault, and industrious as the day is long. Later years fulfilled the promises of his youth. I recollect well, in my younger days, when the young men prided themselves upon their muscle, that none of the boys could run Bill Newby to the shade in harvest times, and few of them craved the other end of his hand-spike at log-rolling.

At the age of twenty-three he left the family hive, selected Fereby Files, the daughter of a neighbor, to join with him in the love and labors of a new home. By his labor and thrift he had raked together enough money to enter five "forties" of government land, and with his ax on his shoulder, and with "Ferebe" and a stout will to back him, he entered his new domain.

"Hard work and hominy," an abundance of rough and healthy food, and of rough, hard labor, growing farm, full barns, increasing thrift, "with now and then a baby to cheer them on their way," sums up his domestic life up to the war.

As to social life in general, the man that is not familiar with the ways of a new country must not imagine for an instant that because men were obliged to work hard for a living, that therefore the people were uninformed and ignorant, and that life was tame and uneventful.

At log-rollings and house-raisings, and at the village gatherings on Saturdays, all questions, public and private, political and religious, were discussed with a vigor and settled with a promptness which often gave many the headache.

At large political gatherings the merits of rival candidates were often settled with fistic arguments inside of a ring of sympathetic partisans. I make the statement on the authority of two distinguished lawyers, one an ex-supreme judge of this state, that fifty fights have been known to occur on a single Saturday during a term of court, and that it was not an uncommon thing to have the court adjourn for a time on account of the fistic discussions on the outside.

The people of that time, as I remember them, were no more brutal than now, but it was the fashion of the times. The moral standard was not so high, perhaps. Men were more of a law unto themselves. I leave this question of comparison to the moralist, however, and simply note the fact that the man that made himself felt in the neighborhood was the man of strong convictions and a strong, sturdy frame. Such a man was William Newby. He was, in politics especially, a man of very strong convictions. And here, for the sake of space and perspicuity, I will drop into the narrative of his old mother.

"William," she said, "was a Whig, but when the war broke out he was a Republican. He was a powerful man for a young man, and he was strong for the Union. All of my boys were. One night his brother-in-law, who was a Southern sympathizer, came along the road by my house and carelessly hollered for Jeff. Davis. William happened to be there unbeknowns to him, and he jumped on his horse, and chased him up the road to chastise him. All my boys were strong Union men. They threatened to hang my oldest son in Jefferson County, and he had to come down here among his friends. William enlisted in the army the 8th day of August, 1861. Three of my boys went off together to the war. I think they went to Camp Butler, Illinois."

This far thirty-five years have passed in this man's life; a life thus far no more eventful than your own or your neighbor's; a life that may be summed up in a very few lines; a life like yours or mine, that might be crowded into an epitaph, thus—

HERE LIES
WILLIAM NEWBY,
Born in Tennessee in 1826,
Moved to Illinois in 1832,
Married Ferba Files, 1849,
Joined the army in 1861,
Was kil— . . ? ? ? ?

But here the pen drops. An apparition arises. It brings with it strange tales. It represents William not as dead, but as very much alive, and walking on the earth these thirty years; walking, not as a disquieted spirit, but in human form— in at least three human forms, so mixed and mingled with each other as to be the impersonation of a great mystery which defies the keenest research, and has heretofore baffled the efforts of the brightest minds.

In the next chapter the reader will see William Newby enrolled, weighed, measured, and placed in the ranks of Company D, 40th Illinois Infantry. When the battle of Shiloh is over, where is he? Killed? and like Lazarus, carried into Abraham's bosom? or disabled? stunned? and, like the rich man, carried (finally) into— Andersonville?

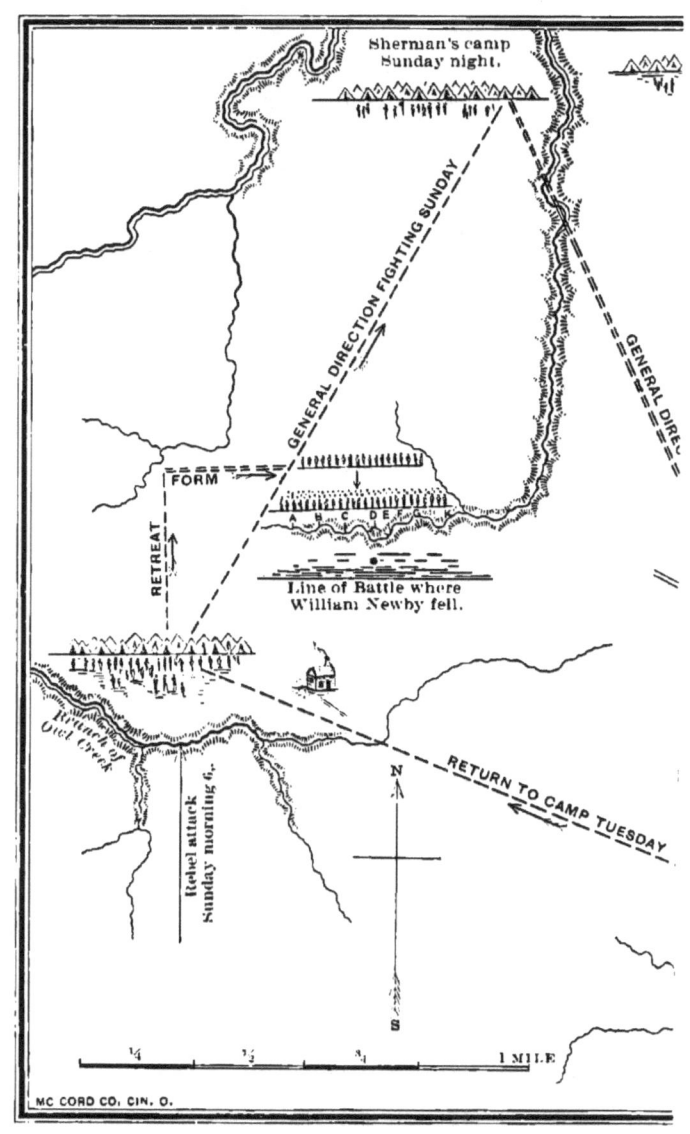

A MAP SHOWING THE POSITION OF COMPANY D AT

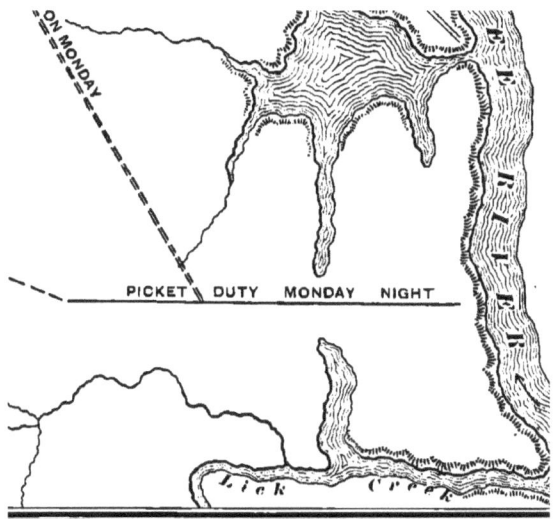

HE BATTLE OF SHILOH, SUNDAY, APRIL 6, 1862.

CHAPTER II.

WAS NEWBY KILLED AT SHILOH?

"WILLIAM NEWBY, age 35; hair dark; eyes gray; height 5 ft. 11 in." Such is the description of William Newby as it appears upon the records of the government when he entered the army in 1861. From Fairfield, where he was enrolled, he went with his company to Camp Butler, thence to Jefferson Barracks, thence to Paducah, Ky., and finally, on Sunday morning, April 6, 1862, we find him with his regiment in Sherman's brigade, in camp a little north of Owl Creek, near Shiloh's meeting-house, answering to roll-call for the last time. The fates were hovering around us. In two hours Death had taken out his toll from our ranks, and Oblivion had marked Newby for his own.

In order to throw some light on the question, "Was Newby killed at Shiloh?" it is proper that I should set forth the events of that day as I saw them; and inasmuch as his post was very near my side I may be as competent to state the part that he took in this engagement as another, and there is no man in the world more desirous to record these events faithfully.

The first question always asked is "Was it a surprise?" For this, every man has his own answer. I am willing to state most positively that I was surprised.

It was on a beautiful sunny morning, April 6, 1862. The reveille had been sounded, the men had answered to their names, and breakfast was in a more or less advanced stage of preparation among the different messes. I was multiplying contrivances to reduce my tincupful of coffee to a drinking temperature, when the bullets began to fall in the camp. This incident, trifling in itself, has always been proof to me "as strong as Holy Writ" that our superior officers did not know that the enemy were moving on us that morning in full force. For my part, I have always regretted that Sherman did not own up to being slipped up on unawares that Sunday morning, or, at least, that it was a surprise in some measure. Picket firing had been going on for a day or two, and we had become somewhat used to the crack of rifles at the front, but here was another state of affairs. Z-z-z-z-p a bullet; z-z-z-z-p another. Here were signs of a real battle—signs as unmistakable as the negro's signs of rain: "Thunder, lightning, and big drops falling in the mill-pond." An "ager," totally unlike the Wabash variety, seized me. The long roll sounded, and the boys fell in. It was our first battle. We faced south, crossed the creek, advanced up the hill, and soon saw the enemy sweeping on to the attack. We were ordered to fall back. We retreat across the creek, pass through our camp and through the woods in as good order as the nature of the case would permit, until we reached a small stream a quarter of a mile back (north) of our camp. In about a half an hour we reform, or, to be accurate, we reassemble. By this time the panicky feeling had passed away, and all the men were full of fight. We were drawn up in line on the brink of a little hill, near a swampy, little creek. It was here, about thirty paces from this stream, that I detailed Sergeant Merritt and R. H. Maricle to take William Watkins, who had just been struck by a stray missile, to a place of safety. This was their principal participation in the battle until their services in burying the dead after the smoke of the battle had cleared away.

After we had reformed we advanced in good order, regiment line of march, east about a quarter of a mile, or about the same distance we had fallen back. Here we were put in line of battle facing south, and were marched about six hundred yards front, where we halted for half an hour on the north side of a crooked little creek or ravine. The enemy were seen pushing through a sage-field in front of us, and we were ordered to charge.

Into the charge we good officers mounted, and the gray-coats charged into the woods and down upon us. Our line of battle was formed, say, seventy-five feet south of the ravine. The companies, as they stood in line of battle, were in alphabetical order, beginning with A on the right, and K on the left, ten companies, letter J being omitted.

The left of Company C would rest on the right of Company D, which was Newby's company, and the right of Company E would rest on the left of D. Remember, they were charging south; the right, or Company A, to the west, and the left, or Company K, to the east. (See map.) The men, coming to the creek, which was very crooked, would tend, more or less, to cross it at right angles, and would be faced east or west, as the crooks or turns might bring them. As the line of battle was only a few steps south of this creek, and as there were trees and logs there, which were used by the soldiers to protect them from the bullets of the enemy, it is easily seen how men belonging to one company would naturally be thrown beside members of adjoining companies on their right or left, and also how men from different companies would be liable to see Newby in or after the fight.

In the arrangement of the men the largest were always at the head of the company next to the orderly sergeant. Adam Files, being the largest, was next to me, then came the three Newby boys, William, James and Whaley, all large men.

Files, the Newbys, and Levi Shores—another large man—pushed about twenty feet ahead of Captain Hooper and myself, and the captain, thinking that they were exposing themselves too much to the enemy, went forward and told them to get down and fight low. Coming back to my side, he turned around, and, seizing my arm, he pointed to Adam Files, who had been instantly killed. Bullets were flying like hail, and in another moment Hooper himself fell at my feet dead. In a few minutes more (I can not tell the exact length of time) I saw William Newby, who had been lying low and firing on the enemy, squirming around on his right side, turning his head to the north, with his hand on his head, and blood flowing from the left side of his head, somewhere above the ear. He was near a tree, by which I think he stopped and ceased his efforts to crawl away. Whaley Newby lost the use of his right arm here. James escaped unhurt, and has since died in Texas.

The fire from the enemy becoming more and more deadly, and the officers and Captain Hooper having been killed, we retreated, leaving seven men on the field.

The question is, was William Newby killed? Marion Files says he saw him by that tree in a sitting posture, and that Newby told him that he was badly hurt, or shot to pieces, or both— he was not certain which.

James Watson saw him after he was shot, and says that he was not shot in the forehead, and that he was not dead when he saw him. Sergeant Rose, John Null, and others, say that they saw him lying on the field, wounded on the side of the head.

William McNeely, who knew Newby, saw the dead about noon on Monday, about twenty-four hours after the battle, and he says that Newby was not one of them.

Peter J. Files, the hospital steward, whose duty it was to look after the wounded, says that Newby was not among the dead on the field on Monday afternoon. He was a brother-in-law to Newby, and a nephew of Adam Files, who was killed within a few feet of where Newby was shot, and whom he recognized. Mr. Files claimed, when the report of the battle was being made up, that we would have to look somewhere else for "Bill." The following is an extract from a letter just received from Mr. Files, which will explain itself.

HEBER, ARK., August 11, 1893.
Comrade G. J. George:
In regard to Bill Newby, I would say that I never saw him after he was shot. You doubtless know that I was on detail in hospital when the battle commenced, but joined the company on the left. Newby was on the right, so I did not see him shot; but after we drove the rebels back on Monday, past where our men were killed, I went back to where our men were killed and wounded, to take them off the field. That was Monday afternoon. I made a diligent search for

Bill Newby, but could not find him. I found all the rest of our dead; I think forty in number. It was easy enough to recognize the dead when I first went back. I always did know our burying party never buried Newby, but supposed he was buried by some other party, for I made diligent search for his body, but it was not anywhere near where any of the rest of the bodies were. It was claimed at the time that he was shot near the bodies of Uncle Ad (Files) and Captain Hooper. I knew that couldn't be so. I see it was sworn to that they turned him over and took a knife and some tobacco out of his pocket. Now, Bill Newby never used tobacco. I am satisfied that I saw the body of Hi Morris on the field. . . . The reason that I was not at trial was, I was away from home, and did not get home until the 19th, and supposed that the trial was over before I knew it was going on.   Yours truly,

PETER J. FILES.

After the battle he wrote to his sister, Mrs. Newby, not to be in a hurry about a pension —that Bill was not found there.

William Murphy, who died about a year ago, told me that he saw Newby after he was shot, sitting up by a tree. Thomas Ellis, who also died about a year ago, said he saw him alive, and knew precisely where he was hit. He was seen by about twelve comrades after he was wounded, but no one claims to have seen him dead on the field of Shiloh. We marched and fought eastwardly along the Purdy road, and at the "Hornet's Nest" we held the enemy at bay until Prentiss was captured, when we retired into camp about a mile back (north) of where we were encamped in the morning.

On Monday morning we faced south again, and struck the enemy on the Purdy road, east of the point of our engagement on Sunday morning. We fought and drove them the next day without further loss, and camped Monday night about three miles southeast of the place where we first saw the enemy. On Tuesday we struck northwestwardly for our old camp, reaching that point about twelve o'clock on Tuesday.

Here the detail was made by me to go and bury the dead who fell on the bank of the ravine. They went and buried them on the afternoon of Tuesday, certainly more than fifty hours after they were killed. These facts are admitted by all except W. H. Merritt, one of the two men who positively swear that they buried Newby, and he claims that he buried him on Monday.

The men detailed went and dug a long ditch, and buried seven, including William Newby.

Did they or did they not? Is it possible that they could be mistaken? I believe now they were. Why? In the first place, we had seen him badly wounded. The impression among the boys was that he was probably killed, and the detail went upon the ground expecting to find him, and was ready to take any large man that might be lying around there for Newby, in the absence of the man himself.

Corpses, dressed alike in blue uniform, that have lain out in the sunshine and rain for nearly two nights and three days, and who are swollen and discolored, are more likely to be identified by their size and general appearance than by any close scrutiny of features. I accompanied the party myself, and saw the work done. The Files boys, sons of "Uncle Ad," who fell first, as before mentioned, being unable to go with the party, gave me a new blanket when we started, and requested me to see that it was placed around their father. I identified him mainly by his size and gray hairs. He, with the others, had lain there two nights and nearly three days, during which time there had been two heavy rains, with sunshine between. His face was black. He was greatly swollen, and the foam was running from his nose and mouth.

Any old soldier understands how this duty of burying the dead is performed. They are not buried as are neighbors at home, with hearse, procession, funeral, and sweet songs.

We must not say that a soldier does not care for a dead soldier, but after a man has stood in the ranks and shot at men for two or three days; has seen his friends crawling around on the ground bleeding like hogs; has seen brother or father fall by his side and give up the ghost with only a hollow groan; when he has made up his mind to share a like fate; when bloodshed and carnage have become familiar sights to eyes, and the cries and moans of the wounded and dying have become familiar sounds to his ears, the man's sensibilities become blunted. Then, after the enemy has been whipped and driven off the ground; when he is tired and worn out with hard fighting, to have to shoulder his spade and go out upon a field where the dead are thicker than sheaves in the harvest field, is, to say the least of it, no labor of love. He looks upon the burial of the dead, not as matter of sentiment, but as a strictly sanitary measure. The truth is, that many times he goes in a perfunctory manner among the blackened corpses, where friends and foes lie together in heaps, digs the trench, and lays or pitches them in, as the case may be. He knows they are indifferent to sentiment, and beyond suffering, so holds no inquest, and pronounces no funeral oration. He rarely gives the men he buries a thought or a look, but feels that the order of the superior officer is executed, and his duty performed, if he puts his fallen comrades away where fowls of the air may not prey upon them and the hogs will not root them up.

Under such circumstances mistakes might easily arise, and many have arisen. I was by, and did not know whether Newby was buried or not, and all the men in the party but two claim that they identified him, and knew that he was buried—W. H. Merritt and Dr. Maricle.

And there are other and very good grounds for believing that Newby was not buried there. As has been stated, Company C was immediately to the right of where Newby stood, and it has been shown that the members of these two companies could have easily been mixed up in this particular place.

There were in Company C two men—"Hi" Morris and "Mi" Morris. "Mi" was killed, and buried. "Hi" was last seen in that charge near Newby. He was not buried by Company C's men. They reported him missing, but he has never been seen or heard of since. The adjutant general's report has it that "Hi" Morris was discharged. This is a mistake. As stated before, he has never been heard of. This is sworn to by all the members of his company, known to be a fact by the whole community. His widow failed to get a pension by reason of the fact stated, and married, and now lives in an adjoining county.

The fact is, as we now believe, the boys thought they buried Newby, but buried "Hi" Morris instead. Another circumstance is worth noting. One of the men who believe that Newby was found dead on the field claims that he turned the body over, and took from his pocket a knife and a plug of tobacco. It is a fact attested by all who knew William Newby that he never used tobacco before the war, nor does he now.

Now as to the testimony of Merritt and Maricle. As stated before, when William Watkins was wounded by a stray shot or shell, these two men were detailed to carry him off to a place of safety. This is the last we saw or heard of them until we finished up our triangular march, and struck the old camp on Tuesday, where we found them.

There seems to be a fatal weakness in the evidence of the first-named gentleman, from the fact that he claims and insists that I told him on Monday that Newby was dead; and he says on oath that he buried him on Monday. This last fact can not be true. The whole trend of the events, as well as the evidence of the other man, Dr. Maricle, and the whole company, is against him. If he was detailed by me at all, it must have been on Tuesday afternoon, when he had no better opportunity of identifying the body than other men.

Dr. Maricle, the most active witness for the government, the strong support of the burying theory—the Atlas on whose shoulders that theory rests—has changed his opinion on the matter twice since Newby came back, and on whichever side you find him you find him an active partisan. At the trial he swore that he knew Newby before the war and in the war. He was not in the battle, but saw him the third day after, when the dead were buried, identified him, and helped to place a board at the head of the grave.

It is singular that a man who has experiences that he is willing to swear to now should have expressed doubts as to those same experiences but a short time ago.

When Newby came home, when he had been examined, and all the marks found upon his person, when his recollection of places and events had proven him to be the veritable man, as will be narrated in the next chapter, Dr. Maricle was one of the first to acknowledge the fact, and one of the loudest in proclaiming it to the world. Mrs. Newby, whose family physician he had been for many years, was in Texas visiting, and the doctor, in his enthusiasm, hastened to send her a long telegram, stating that her lost husband had returned, and tells her to come home and "help kill the fatted calf." This he followed up with a six-page letter, setting forth the facts of the discovery of her husband and his restoration to his home. He apologized for the great mistake he had made in supposing that he had buried the man at Shiloh, congratulated her on his return, and urged her to come home and join him.

Maricle was a big man in the neighborhood. He was her doctor, and confidential adviser in many things. She believed in him, and on the strength of these positive statements and these appeals, she came home. She met Newby, recognized him on sight, and accepted him as her long-lost husband of her own accord.

The fact that Maricle did preach, argue, and contend that the returned man was William Newby was notorious throughout the neighborhood, and his zeal in promulgating the fact was equaled only by that of Presley Newby, his brother-in-law, and brother of William Newby.

The telegram and letter, although denied by him until produced in court, was finally acknowledged by him to be genuine.

"What reason," you inquire, "does he give for his alleged belief in Newby, and for the writing of this letter?"

The excuse he gives is, that he was afraid of the Newby boys.

Think of this a little.

If he did not believe it was Newby, could he not have lain low and said little, and thus avoided their alleged hostility?

Why should boys, peaceable as they are known to be, and who had never known their father, have had convictions so strong as to make it dangerous for their neighbors to differ from them?—at a time, too, when they were awaiting the return of their mother to learn from her whether it was their father or not.

It is not claimed by Maricle that they stood over him with pistol or bludgeon and forced him to write that six-page letter. The U. S. mail is private, and a man can write what he pleases, and he did write that letter voluntarily, and the contents were what he chose to make them.

He could have informed her in that letter that there was a man in that neighborhood claiming to be her husband; that there were some singular circumstances connected with the case; that the boys were of the opinion that he was their father, but that he himself had grave doubts about it. He could have done this without danger, and if he had been honest, and believed what he says he did, he would probably have advised her to come home and settle the point, but to use great caution in the matter. All this he could have said on one sixth of the paper he did use, and yet have taken no chances of being injured by the boys.

What did he do?

On his own confession in court, he wrote a long letter to the gray-haired old widow, his old neighbor, whose confidential adviser he had been for years, urging her to come home—for what? To take to herself, in the place of her husband, whom he knew to be dead, a miserable old tramp; to live with him in adultery the rest of her days; to take upon herself the care and burden of a decrepit old man for the rest of her natural life. He deliberately tried to inflict upon the Newbys a state of affairs that was liable at any time in the future to breed a miserable scandal which would destroy the peace and happiness of that innocent family. The course pursued by him certainly lays him open to criticism. The reason he gives for that course is an ugly reflection upon himself, and an insult to the intelligence of the community around him.

The community will not accept his reason, and gives what it considers a better one. Dr. Maricle, it is claimed, desired to be conspicuous in the matter, and there began to be friction as soon as the Newbys signified their intention to look after their own interests.

It began to be hinted that it was worth something to stand by a man who wanted friends to assist him in getting a pension with back pay. Doubts soon began to gather over the minds of the doctor and Presley in regard to the identity of Newby. Presley became so "jubious" about its being brother Bill that he declared that it would take five hundred dollars to make him stand by him.

The Newby folks were not disposed to make any bargains, and, without leave or license from the brother-in-laws, went to McLeansboro and filed their application.

Here was a state of affairs not to be tolerated. The old lady had taken his advice and medicine for years; he had spent his time and good money in getting her to come back from Texas, and he now proposed to be consulted. If the widow and the boys were going to ignore him and Pres, they were stout enough to knock the bottom out of the whole thing. He was influential, and had been very active in maintaining that it was Newby, while Presley had never ceased to proclaim it since he had come home, and now if they should go square back on him, they could twist public opinion around the other way. The scandal-mongers would raise the howl, Newby would be run out of the settlement, the public would point the finger of scorn at the old widow, whom he had gotten into the trouble, and he could say to her, "I told you so."

As to the telegram and letter, that was a mistake. But had not Henry Clay, Blaine, Hancock, and other great men, made the same kind of a mistake? He could deny it as long as possible, and then say that he was afraid of the boys.

The case, stated bluntly by those who think they know, is simply this: These men thought that the Newbys were not going to "tote fair" with them in the matter of the pension, and they proceeded to jump on the old man with both feet to crush him.

It may be stated here that whatever the motive may have been, their turning had no such effect. There was no turning of public opinion, and no collapse except in the prestige, practice, and pill-bags of the doctor himself.

In concluding this chapter, I will say that in consideration of the fact that no one saw William Newby killed; considering the length of time that elapsed between the engagement and the time of the alleged burial; the liability of mistakes under such circumstances, as shown by other cases cited in this book; the character of the testimony on both sides—taking all things into consideration—there is a presumption, amounting to a strong probability, that he was not buried at the time alleged, and subsequent developments will show conclusively, I think, that William Newby was not killed at Shiloh.

REBECCA NEWBY ("MAMMY").

CHAPTER III.

RETURN OF WILLIAM NEWBY.

THE work of burying our comrades at Shiloh was done—done, perhaps, with some tenderness, but without any tears—buried as soldiers bury soldiers—roughly.

Afterwards we piled the rebel dead in pits, shouldered our spades, and left them, friend and foe, to rest in peace, until the great roll-call in the hereafter.

Ten, twenty, nearly thirty years have come and gone to join the years beyond the flood.

For a quarter of a century peace and prosperity have blessed the land.

The wife of William Newby, now a grayhaired grandmother, still lives on the old farm, and the children have built themselves homes of their own.

So the year 1891 finds them.

Then comes the strange rumor that William Newby is still alive. Old army men have detected in the ungainly figure of a traveling mendicant the wreck of the once manly Newby. His gait all broken up, his whole frame threatening to fall to staves, seemingly, with barely sense enough to tell his name, to ask for bread, or to pilot him from one poorhouse to another, yet, under this ruin of mind and body, Newby stands confessed.

From the general appearance of the man they conclude that he must be William Newby. They ask his name, and he says that it is William Newby, and that he was wounded at Shiloh, and carried away prisoner by rebels. His reason seemed to be made of the stuff that dreams are made of—flitting, fantastic, with now and then a real picture from the store-house of memory.

What he did know and what he did not know were unaccountable alike.

Many strange chapters have been written concerning the effects of injury to the brain. Why, if he knew himself to be Newby, did he not go home? This we can no more tell than we can tell why a fever will cause you, my reader, to shrink in terror from the wife that bends over you to bathe your burning brow. Why should he have those old dreams of the past? This we can no more answer than we can tell why, in the hour of dissolution, when oblivious to what is passing around them, the dying mutter strange things, and talk of the companions of their early youth and childhood. However strange seemed his conduct, the fact remained that he resembled the man, and knew many things that only Newby could know.

Thoroughly convinced that some great mistake had been made, he was sent to the poorhouse in his own county, White, and his friends informed of the facts here stated.

We will here turn him over to his friends, and our pen to the shorthand-writer, and let them tell in their own words the story of the capture and restoration to his home, and the gradual dawning of his reason, or rather the brightening of his recollection when brought in contact with the surroundings of his youth.

From the hundreds of circumstances that might be cited to show the nature of the evidence upon which the friends of the unfortunate man base their faith in his being the man we claim him to be, I will give the reader a sufficient number to give food for thought, and if he can digest and explain these away, he would be able to dispose of the balance.

Hezekiah Newby, or "Ki," as he is generally called, is an active young farmer, the son of William Newby, living a half mile from the old homestead, and a fac-simile of the father when he enlisted in the army before the war. When asked about the particulars of the discovery and return of his father he said:

"The very first I knew of the matter was this: I met Jess Talkington one day, and he told me that Newt Moutry told him that William Newby was alive, and not dead. I says, 'No, sir, it can't be so, because he's dead and buried too long.' But that night at supper I asked John Kennett if it was possible for people to be fooled in burying a man. He said, 'Yes, in war, when they are shot, they soon turn black as a hog.' I says, 'Talkington reports that father is living; he says that Newt Moutry was over at McLeansboro, and brought the word over, and Jess told him he would tell some of the boys about it.'

"So the next morning I started to McLeansboro to find the men that said he was father. The men were Crede Lay, Allen Baine, Mose Robinson, and John B. Smith. They said they knew him in the war, saw him about the time he was shot, knew him then, and knew him now. Some of them told me that there had been sworn statements in regard to this being William Newby, and I went from there to Carmi, Ill., and I found him in the White County poorhouse. He was out in the back yard, and they called for William Newby. He came in and claimed to be William Newby. I remarked that this man had the Newby foot, and was Newby from the chin up. I talked a little with him, and I saw that he had the Newby features by the rest of the family, including a big No. 10 foot. After I had interviewed him, I went back to Carmi and went back home to see Uncle Whale Newby, to see him and his brothers, that I might get them and bring them where they might see him and know whether he was the real, identical Newby or not. I was doing it in behalf of my mother, Ferby Newby. I thought it might be an impostor, and might get her pension away from her. She was out in the state of Texas, and she might not know what checked it.

"The family had heard of the report, and knew that I had been down there, and the family had got together and drawn their conclusions on the questions as to the marks that were on him when he left, that they all knew of.

"When I got home Uncle Pres stated to me that there was a mark made by the kick of a colt on his shin, and also a mark on his foot, cut by a broadaxe, a mole on the corner of the mouth, a mole on the temple, a slight cut above the knee by a drawer-knife, and tooth-marks on the arm where old Whout Gray bit him.

"After I had started to the poorhouse in White County, Uncle Whaley and my brother had gone there too, and I passed them on the side track as I came home, not knowing it. When they went down there the man was gone. They came back, and Whaley contended that from the description they gave him at the poorhouse it must be Carroll Newby, another brother. He thought Carroll was personating William Newby, and says he, 'I wouldn't have him do that for my farm.' Him and me and young Tullis started together to find father. All the way Uncle contended that I was mistaken, and that it was nobody else than Carroll Newby. I told him that I knew Carroll as well as I did myself, and when we found him it wasn't Carroll Newby by a good deal. We started on the trail at the county farm. We went west and then south, and then we went an angling direction to New Haven, then in a northern direction. When we got eight or nine miles from New Haven we lost the trail, and I proposed that we make a circle and make an old-fashioned drive like blood hounds. By making about a three-mile circle we found the trail again. We took an east direction and ran him to the Wabash. The Wabash was high, out of its banks, and we caught up with him off the road at a farm house. We had hunted him two days and had traveled about twenty-five miles, and was then about nineteen miles from Carmi.

"We looked for all these marks and scars that Uncle Pres had stated were on him, and found them all on the very particular places where he had made his statements, and then we decided that he was no one else but the real William Newby, and then proposed to bring him home, after examining him.

"He says, 'How in the hell are you going to take me? What will you do for something to ride?' I remarked that I was ordinarily stout, and could walk and change with one of the others. We did this way till we got to Hamilton, then Uncle Whaley took the train. My mother being in Texas, I brought him to my house the first night. The next day I took him over to the original old home. I said, 'Now, this is your old home.' He says, 'The ground looks natural, but the building don't look natural.' We had built a big story-and-a-half frame on the front and porch where he said he only had two cabin houses. He said he never put that house there, which was true. I asked him if he had built the brick chimney at the old log house. He said, 'I had nothing but stick and clay chimneys, and if it's my log house it has béen put there since I left.' This was true, too. I was trying to play it on him. I wanted to know if he knowed. I took him around to the northwest corner of the house, and asked him if he remembered the old cistern. He looked down and says, 'No, by G—, I never dug that.' Then he looked around and says, 'This is not the cistern;' he says, 'this cistern is in a southeast direction, and is not the cistern I dug, for the one I dug was in a northwestern direction, and may be filled up if there ain't any there, but I never dug this one.' The one that he says he dug was actually there, and is there yet, at the very place he says he dug it. He had never seen the place till I took him to it.

"He says to me, 'The barn looks like it is in the right direction from the house, but the roof looks like it has been turned half around, running the water-troughs westward. It used to be running troughs south. It sits about where it used to sit. It may be a short distance east,' which is as true as anybody on God's green earth could have told it if he had been there every day since he left.

"I was trying him on my own knowing. I wanted to write to ma, and I wanted to write the truth. I was afraid that he was an impostor.

"He says, 'Here is the barn and here is the orchard. It don't look natural on the west because it has been cleared up now where it was in timber when I left.'

"A woman named Amanda Haines, who was living on the place at the time, said to him, 'Do you know what I was doing when you passed our house at John Files, when you were going to the war?' He said, 'I don't know exactly what you was doing, but the old Missus Files was picking geese.' And she was picking geese at the barn the last time he was there till now.

"The next day I went with him to Uncle Jim Files'. Jim says, 'Well, Bill, do you know anything about anything here?' And he says, 'I don't know, I will look.' Files asked him if he could remember anything about his house and barn. And Bill says, 'If I understand anything I know, your barn was a round-log barn and not a frame barn, and it was in a south direction from this house.' We asked him if there was anything else he could locate. Says he, 'What became of that spring out this way?' pointing west from the house. He goes to where he thought the spring was, and looked for it and could not find it. He says it used to run out and over this bank and into the creek, and now it don't do that way. Files had a ten-bushel box turned over it, and he could not find the spring at all, but after he had looked all around for it, like he was looking for a rat, he said, 'I can't find it.' Files said, 'Lift the lid of that box and look in.' He did so, and said, 'My God, it's walled now; when I left, it had puncheons over it,' which was true, but Files had forgotten it himself.

"Then I taken dinner, and went over to the old farm where he was raised. We went out on the old place. Where the house is now is a little bit northwest from where the old stood, and going over on the field we came to it. He said, 'My God, here is the very spot where mother's old house used to be. This is the old chimney-place, and over yonder is the old fireplace. Someone said, 'Is that all you recollect?' He says, 'Well, no; there was a cistern a few steps in an eastern direction.' They told him to hunt for it, and he gave it up and says, 'By G——, it's filled up.' The boys began to laugh, and says, 'You're mistaken in the place.' He says, 'No, I aint; I would know those old chimneys anywhere.' (These were about the only brick chimneys in that neighborhood in that day.) He said, 'I know what I am talking about, for I have been here too often not to know what I do know.' Then he began looking, and the boys says, 'Bill, look under that rail pile, and see if there is not a rat under it.' He threw off some rails and says, 'By G——, here's that old cistern.' The place was covered with weeds and sticks. They asked him if he knew where the gate was. He says, 'No, I don't; there never was a gate here; it was an old-fashioned pair of draw-bars.' Pointing, he says, 'There is where the bars used to be, but no gate at all,' and showing us in the direction where the road used to run years ago, where there is now a ditch twenty-five feet wide, taking in the entire road now, and ten feet deep, he said, 'There is where the road was, for I remember the road when I left here.'"

These incidents are set down to show the manner of Newby's introduction to his home, and the methods employed to identify him, and the result. The results, in general, were that he located places and recalled facts and circumstances relating to the surroundings of the old home that had been forgotten by other members of the family.

Thirty years of the dog-life that he had lived and the half demented condition of his mind had left their impress on his face, and the effect of the bullet-wound on the skull had changed his once strong regular gait into an indescribable teetering motion, painful and wonderful to see; so that, to some, the appearance of the old ruin of sixty-six failed to recall the robust young man of thirty, but there were the marks and scars on his person; there were the "Newby features from the chin up," including a "No. 10 foot," as "Ki" put it; there was the man walking, or shambling, about the place, describing things as they existed long ago, precisely as William Newby would have done it.

However unreal and unreasonable the things might seem, with these facts before them there was no denying that the man was Newby.

It will be proper to remark here that all these incidents were ruled out at the trial, the witness being only allowed to state when on this line that he believed the person to be Newby by reason of his remembering certain circumstances, but was not allowed to particularize. This ruling is said by lawyers to be an unusual one in such cases, but whether it be in accordance with the rules of evidence in the courts or not, I propose to give a few of them to the public.

Being desirous of getting the facts at first hands from members of the family, I called at the home of Andy Tullis, a substantial farmer and a perfectly reliable man, a brother-in-law to the Newbys. The old mother and two sisters of William Newby were present at the interview.

I said, " Mr. Tullis, I want you to state the facts concerning the return of William Newby, and tell me what led you to conclude that it was William Newby."

He said, " William Newby returned on the 13th or 14th day of April, 1892, to Ki Newby's house. In the afternoon of that day we were all together for the purpose of settling the question of whether it was Bill or not. Presley Newby examined him mostly, and the first question he asked was, ' Did you ever raft logs any?'

" He said, ' Yes.'

" ' Where ? '

" ' Out of the White River into the Arkansas, with my brother Jim.'

"'Was there any extraordinary circumstances happened while you were down there?'

"'Yes.'

"'What was it?'

"'An Irishman died of the yellow fever, and they called upon me to shave him, supposing him dead. I commenced shaving him, and before I was half done the man lifted up one of his arms. I dropped the razor and jumped back, for I was scared. It was some time before I finished shaving him after I found out he was dead for certain.'"

The old lady Newby, sitting by Mr. Tullis, stated that this happened forty-four years ago, and that her sons Jim and William had talked about it many a time after they came home from that trip. She also stated that her son Jim died twelve years ago in Texas.

"The next question that Presley asked him," continued Tullis, was, 'What did you do with your raft?'

"'Took it out of White River into a big river and took it down to New Orleans.'

"'Did anything happen to the raft?'

"'Yes, the raft broke in two, and we lost it.'

"'What is the reason you did not come home? You stayed nearly nine months on that trip.'

"'The principal reason was that Jim wanted to join the regular army, and I didn't want him to do it because I knew if I came home without Jim that Mammy would never forgive me.'

"'What else happened?'

"'I took the yellow fever, and an old Dutch woman cured me. Then we both took a notion to come home. When we got home, Mammy, she wanted to hug me, and made a fuss over me. Jim wouldn't be hugged, and he climbed up on the lot fence, and Mammy went and hugged his legs.'

The old mother being present at this interview with Tullis, I asked her if this was true. She, and other members of the family present, stated that the thing happened in just that way. She said, moreover, that Bill's eyes were yellow from the effects of the fever when he came home.

Tullis: "Presley's next question was to Bill, 'Have you ever fit [fought] any?'

"'Yes, when I was young I would rather fight than eat. I had two fights.'

"'Where did you have those two fights?'

"'I had a fight in a little town east of here (pointing toward Liberty). I had another fight in a meadow.'

"'Oh, no,' said Presley, 'it was in a wheat-stubble field.'

"James Fenton was present, and said, 'No, Pres, he is right; it was in my meadow."

* * * * * * *

Mr. Tullis stated that after the conversation had been carried on in this manner at considerable length, they all went out over the old places, and he corroborates the statement of " Ki " as to the ability of Newby to describe the premises as they once were.

Mr. Tullis tells this singular circumstance which occurred. He said, "I took him down to see my wheat. It was April, and we went away down in the field. We walked east until the family graveyard was right north. Says I, 'Lets go back.' We had to pass the graveyard, and it was grown up thick with brush. Says I, 'Bill, do you ever have any sassafras in the South?' He says, 'Lots of it.' We were passing through it. We got through the brush, and came in sight of his father's grave, say within fifteen or twenty feet. He raised his hands, and says: 'My daddy's grave.' He went up to it, and sort of half around it, and cried. I saw tears run down his cheeks.

"We said, 'What did your father die of?'

"'He died of consumption, and my brother Carroll and I hauled these rocks'" (referring to large stones five or six feet by two and one half, set on edge around the grave).

Both these statements were true.

Said Mr. Tullis, "My son, who went with Ki Newby to find his father, asked William, as they were returning, if he ever knew a man by the name of Alexander Tullis. He said, 'Yes, I remember about him. He was a Scotchman. He was a school-teacher, and a good school-teacher, too. He was a tall, slim man, and had spots on his face. He had a tolerable big nose and tolerable long teeth,'" a description which fit Tullis exactly.

"Notwithstanding all these things," said Tullis, "I was slow to decide in the matter. I did not want to be the means of bringing a strange, uncouth man into the family unless we were absolutely certain that he was the man, and so Presley Newby came over nearly every day to convince me. Once he says to me, 'What do you think William said to me? He asked me (Presley) what had become of that old walnut trough that we used to beat apples in for cider, and,' said Presley, 'I had forgotten all about the trough myself.'

"I told Pres that I had it. It had been left on the old place. It got old and spilled corn, and I told the boys to make stove-wood of it. It was a big walnut trough, and went the whole length of the sixteen-foot stable."

The mother and sister of Newby were present at this interview and gave their assent to the statements of Mr. Tullis all through.

Turning to the old lady, now over ninety-one years old, I said, "Grandma, where did you first meet your son William when he came back?"

"The first time I saw William after he got back was at Marion Newby's, his son Marion Newby's. I was down there, and they had sent for him. Late in the evening he came from Liberty. He came in at the door, and saw me at the table, and knew me to be his mother. He came in and told me 'Howdy,' and I says to him, 'How did you know it was me?'

"He said, 'I looked in, and saw you at the far corner of the table, and I told them that mother had a red head.'

"He sat down right beside me, and I took his hand, and I told him how many tears that I had shed for that hand.

"He said, 'I got my hand bloody, and I reckon that's the way it got out.' He said, 'I have suffered a heap since I saw you,' and I said, 'I reckon you have.'

"He took up my hand, and put my finger to his mouth and said, 'Mammy, don't you recollect when I had that tooth pulled.' I did not remember it till he told me that he said when he came home, 'I thought that my head would come off.' I told him that Ferebe (his wife) had the tooth yet.

"He said to me, 'Mammy, I had forgot that I ever had a wife or child.' I said, 'Poor fellow, you had?' He said, 'Yes.' I said, 'Yes, you had a wife and children, for I have lived with her.' He said, 'Did she treat you good?' I said, 'Yes, as good as if I was her own mother.' He says, 'I am glad of it.' He says, 'They say she has gone to Texas' (she was in Texas then). He says, 'Mammy, do you reckon that she will like me, or that she will live with me?' 'Yes,' I says, 'she will live with you, William, and be glad to see you.'"

To record the incidents showing the man's wonderful knowledge of the past would be a task as endless as it would be useless.

James Files, a neighbor of Newby's before the war and now, relates this circumstance:

"In early times in the large bottoms in the West Forks it was common for the farmers to have 'wild-hog claims,' which carried with them the title to all hogs running wild within his territory. The leader and protector of this gang, usually an old sow, would wear a bell. Long before the war, a man named Arbaugh had an old sow, which, with her litter of pigs, was in the habit of burglarizing Bill's cornfield. Bill got tired of it, and killed the old sow, and threw her into the creek, bell and all. I was a witness to the fact, but the thing had nearly passed out of my mind, and I had never mentioned the circumstance to anyone. Since Bill came back I was walking with him down the bank one day, when he suddenly turned to me and said, 'I wonder if old Arbaugh ever got his bell out of the creek?'"

The reader will see that the question implied that Newby knew of the circumstance itself; that he knew that Files knew it, and that he knew that Files knew that he knew it.

I will here close with a bit of my own experience with Newby, which is a good sample of all the rest:

I had been wishing to have an opportunity to have a conversation with Newby when he was quiet, not for the purpose of convincing myself that it was Newby, but to test his memory in things that occurred before he left home for the war. I being raised close to him until I was eighteen years old, and being often in his company. I sat down by him one day, and we talked about entering land under the graduation act of 1852. He entered five forties from the government, as heretofore mentioned, and he "entered some squatters out," as he stated it.

I asked him whom he entered out.

He said, "It was Canada and the Taylors."

I said, "No, it was the McNights and Canada. That's my recollection about it."

He said, "No, it was the Taylors, and they're all mad about it yet."

Not long ago, I saw Sam Taylor at Springfield, where he was a witness against Newby, and I asked him if Newby entered him out in 1852.

And he said with much emphasis, "He did that."

At the time of my conversation with Newby he said to me, "Did you ever know who burned Canada's tan-bark."

(This tan-bark was stacked upon the land he had entered from Canada, and was burned in about 1853.) I informed him that I did not know, but that I had not thought of the matter for many years, and asked him if he knew.

He said, "Only three men ever knew who burned it, and one of them is dead. The man that burned it is not dead. I will never tell who burned it unless he dies before I do. Old Sam Marshall," he said, "told the man that burned it that the crime never run out."

He asked me what became of the Fox land, and who now owned it. This land cornered with Newby's land. He said somebody had cut the timber off. He said Fox went with him to Shawneetown at the time that he entered that land (which I know to be true), and he left the money with old Goodrich to pay the taxes, and he had never heard of him up to the time of the war (which I also know to be true).

He said that my father, Frank George, had the best work oxen of anybody in the country. He said the blue steers were the best yoke he ever saw. He said that one time he saw Ratcliff, my brother, hitch them to a heifer of Ed Brown's to pull her out of the mire, and that he told Brown and Ratcliff that the steers would kill the heifer. Brown said, "Let them kill her; we can't get her out any other way." They pulled her out all right, but she bawled and scared the oxen and they ran off and broke her neck. I will state that I was present when the incident occurred, and that Ed Brown has been dead for thirty years, and Ratcliff George died before Newby came back.

Incidents like these could be multiplied indefinitely.

A canvas of the country in which William Newby lives would bring to light scores of instances such as these, more than enough to convince the inquirer that one of three things must be true:

Firstly, that a majority of the people in that part of the country are double-breasted, robust liars; or

Secondly, that the old doctrine of metempsychosis, or the transmigration of souls, is true, and that the spirit of William, finding an earthly vessel, a man marked and scarred as he himself was, the counterpart of his old self while in the body, has taken up his abode therein, and walks among men and talks to them of his mortal experiences; or,

Thirdly, the man is William Newby himself.

KI NEWBY, SON OF CLAIMANT.

CHAPTER IV.

SCARS AS A MEANS OF IDENTIFICATION.

IT has been noted in summing up the results of the trial of claimant that the court, in its ominous leaning, did not call the attention of the jury to the marks and scars on the person of the claimant. These scars were often and most particularly referred to by many of the witnesses on both sides of the case. It has been remarked by a learned legal author, Harris (Law of Identity), that "people are much more similar than we always remember," not disputing the idea existing in so many countries, and which has been the basis of so many fables, that "every man has his double on the face of the earth."

" The changes produced by time renders personal appearance the most difficult of identification. We separate from a friend in youth; years go by, and we bear his image on the tablet of our memory; meet again in old age, and there is a mutual surprise to see the changes wrought by the ruthless hand of Time, and yet there is an indescribable something by which you recognize him. From general characteristics, from family peculiarities or resemblances, you may identify him with reasonable but perhaps not absolute certainty. But if there be any distinctive marks or scars upon him, or moles upon his person, or cuts with axe or adze, known to you, and they are found on him located as of old, then comes a corresponding increase of assurance, and you identify him with great certainty. And when you converse with him, if you narrate incidents of boyhood days, the reminiscences of youth, the sports at gatherings, hunting and fishing, remembers the dogs, horses and oxen, and their names, the old neighbors, where they lived, whom they married, and how many children they had, and their names, the assurance then becomes so full that you identify with absolute certainty. Without peculiarities, marks and scars, rigidly scrutinized, you would have failed in your identification."

"It is wonderful," says the same writer, "to think that all the differences in the faces of the human race are crowded together within a narrow compass, say within the limit of six by ten inches, and all the main features—brow, nose, mouth, eyes, cheeks, and chin—are constructed essentially on the same general pattern." But what a marvelous wealth of difference underlies all this uniformity. Among all faces of the human race no two can be found so nearly alike but that there are persons who may identify them. They look for the scars, the marks, the moles, listen to the voice. The nose is aquiline, Roman, or pug, we know not why, but they know. The marks and scars upon animals and men have been recognized by people of all ages as means of identity, whether natural or accidental. The claimant in this narrative seems to have been marked and scarred especially for some such experience in life as he has encountered.

To call your attention to the rarity of scars in any specified place, and to further suggest their value as a means of identification, I will submit this proposition:

I will ask you, reader, to find me a man with a scar on the left side of his head, three inches above, and one inch behind the ear. I will ask you to find a man who, besides having the wound designated, is marked with another scar on the left foot three inches long?

Study for a moment and decide how many men you will be likely to examine before you strike a man characterized by both of these marks.

Add to these two more scars, one on the right knee, shaped like a half moon, another on the shin. Add to these a mole on the left cheek, and tooth-marks on the left arm.

What will you take to find a man so marked?

What length of time do you want in which to find him?

This is a plain question of probabilities, a department of mathematics upon which such things as life insurance and fire insurance are based, and it is therefore a rational question to consider.

What are the probabilities that such a man marked that way could be found in a lifetime, or in the world?

I verily believe that but one man lived at the beginning of the war with all these marks (except the scar on the head), and that man was William Newby. I believe that there is but one man in the world to-day marked in that way (including the scar on the head), and that man claims to be William Newby, and says that the scar on the head is from a bullet wound received at Shiloh. (It was on "Crazy Jack" at Andersonville.)

MARKS OF IDENTIFICATION. 63

On the first Sunday after Newby was brought home, as related in the previous chapter, there being much excitement in the country, I went to see him. I asked Thomas Ellis, whom I have mentioned as knowing precisely where Newby was wounded, to go with me. He could not go at that time, but told me to take notice, and if the person did not have a scar on the left side of his head about three inches above and one inch behind the ear, that it was not Newby, and if I so reported, that he would not go to see him.

I drove ten miles, and found the unfortunate man at his brother Presley's house. It was Sunday morning, and hundreds had arrived at the place, and carriages and horsemen were pouring over the hills from all directions.

When I arrived at the door, someone remarked, "There is the officer who buried him; let him talk to him."

I sat down by his side, and asked him one question. He looked exhausted and haggard, and complained of being very tired. He had his hat on. I raised his hat, and was startled at the sight of a scar about the size of a half dollar, just where Ellis said it would be if it was Newby. I immediately went out of the house, followed by

Pres and Whale Newby. I said nothing to them about seeing the scar. Whaley said, "Brother Bill looks awful." I remarked that it was a strange business.

"Yes," said Presley, "it's my b-b-brother B-B-ill." (The Newbys all have an impediment in their speech.)

"Then," said I, "You are both satisfied that it is Bill?"

Said Pres, "When Whaley and Ki (Newby's sons) went to hunt for him, I said, 'Now, Whaley, if he haint got a scar on his left foot on the side three inches long, cut with a broadaxe, hewing logs, and one on his shin where a horse kicked him, as big as a half dollar, and one on the opposite knee, cut with a drawer (drawing) knife like a half moon, and a mole on his left cheek as big as a buckshot, and tooth-marks on his left arm, where old Whout Gray bit him in a fight, don't bring him back.'"

I said, "Pres, has he got them on him now?"

He replied, "He has, and he is my brother Bill," and tears came to his eyes as he talked of the condition of his mind and body, and the manner in which he had been treated.

I immediately left the place, satisfied that those two men were not mistaken as to the man being their brother.

Now, a moment's consideration of the proposition in this chapter will show the utter improbability of finding a man having two or three, not to say five or six, peculiar markings in as many different places.

It follows, then, that the man that we claim to be William Newby is William Newby, or that some creature has submitted to being mutilated, maimed, and scarified in order to personate Newby, and only Presley Newby and the other members of the family knew of the scars when he entered the army, and the information could only come from them, and Pres Newby is now against him.

The vital importance of the scars on the claimant is recognized by the government. You will remember that McBride, the special detective and examiner, took Newby to Nashville, Tenn., for inspection and examination, though they evidently did not strip the old fellow, because they came to the trial from Tennessee only prepared for one scar, the one on the head, mentioned by Ellis in this chapter. That scar can be seen at any time when his hat is removed; all other scars and wounds (except the mole) are hid by his clothing. Hence, they proceed to fix that scar, and this by the following process:

About the year 1859 there lived a man by the name of Ally on the Granny White Pike below Nashville, who made wagon-bows by shaving and splitting them out of white oak and then putting them in what they said was a "bender," and the said old man Ally, having a bow in too much of a "bender," it kicked out and hit Dan Benton on the left side of the head, where you can now plainly locate the place of the scar. The three Ally boys swear that they, with Dan, were standing near the "bender," and they all said it made a scalp-wound, and did not stop Dan from "wobbling" around. This was thirty-four years ago.

Query: Would the scar have been accounted for if McBride had not taken Newby to Tennessee?

Alas! this scar on the head of this once powerful man is why this book is written. It is the preface. By that sliver from the skull, that injury to the brain and nerve, this man lost more than life—his reason. He is thereby compelled to ask the government to excuse him for the many unaccountable things he has since unknowingly done.

CHAPTER V.

PARALLEL CASES.

J. C. SMITH,
65 SIBLEY STREET, CHICAGO.

N. E. Roberts, Fairfield, Ill.

DEAR SIR: I am directed by Gen. Smith to forward to you the inclosed letter, also check No. 2,189 for $5, to be used in the "William Newby Defense Fund."

Very truly yours,
J. C. SMITH, JR.

CHICAGO, ILL., August 8, 1893.

MY DEAR FRIEND ROBERTS: Enclosed please find a small contribution to the fund for the defense of William Newby, and I thank you for the noble stand you have taken in his behalf. I am unable to see how anyone could doubt the evidence as to the identity of Comrade Newby, much less have "a reasonable doubt" as to the defendant being Dan. Benton. I feel a deep interest in this case, the more so that one of my own soldiers might easily have been in the sad plight of William Newby, and now be proven someone else other than himself.

As the Chief of Staff of General James B. Stedman, I received a report of the casualties of his division in the battle of Chickamauga, including my own regiment, the 96th Illinois Infantry. The original reports of all the regiments are still in my possession, copies having been made and forwarded to department headquarters and the war department. In the list of dead of Company A of the 96th Illinois appears the name of Josephus Metcalf, who was seen by the officers and members of his company to have fallen in a charge, pierced through the brain with a bullet. On that report his widowed mother applied for his back pay and bounty, which I believe was settled, and made application for pension. While this was in process of adjustment Joseph Metcalf came back to his regiment, an exchanged prisoner of war. It proved that the bullet which struck him in center of the forehead, from which blood was seen to flow, and which had rendered Metcalf insensible, was a spent ball, and it was only when about to be buried by the enemy that he returned to consciousness.

Discovering that Private Metcalf was not strong, and it being feared that his mind was impaired, he was assigned to light duty, and finally to guard some company property from Nashville to Chattanooga. More than one year after his injuries at Chickamauga, while on this duty, he fell from the train, and was sent to the hospital adjoining the Chattanooga depot in Nashville, and there again died. His final statements were received by his captain from the surgeon in charge, sent to me then in Nashville, and on going to the hospital to see about his effects I found Joe Metcalf alive and hobbling about on crutches. On the muster-out of the regiment, Comrade Metcalf returned to his old home in Galena, and being a Mississippi River steamboat engineer, he engaged in that occupation, as he had done before the war. His conduct, however, was so erratic that he could not keep a boat long, and was shifted about from one to another. Three attempts at suicide failed, one of which was the cutting of a vein in his arm while at the hotel in Dunleith—now called East Dubuque; again at Prairie du Chien he took arsenic, but being discovered each time the physicians saved him.

Sitting in my office one day, in Galena, Captain Augustus Esty, president of the Merchants'

National Bank of that city, entered, saying, "General, I saw one of your soldier boys dead at Shullsburg, Wis., yesterday." I asked who, and he replied: "Joseph Metcalf." The captain then went on to tell me that Metcalf had entered a drug-store, purchased a quantity of strychnine, saying that he wanted to kill some dogs near a mine where he was running an engine, and being well known, it was unhesitatingly given to him. Upon receiving the strychnine he asked for a drink of water, and, taking it in one hand and the poison in the other, saying, "Now you will see a dead man in less time than you ever saw one before," swallowed each, and commenced to walk toward the door, but fell dead before he reached it. Captain Estey saw the body placed in a wagon, to be taken to the mine where he had worked, and then left for his home in Galena, coming to see me the next day, when he related the above story. During the same day John Combellick, the owner of a smelting furnace in East Galena, also came into my office, and informed me that the day before he had been to Shullsburg, Wis., to purchase mineral, and then related the same story as to the death of Metcalf.

No longer doubting the death of the brave but

unfortunate soldier, I wrote his obituary for the Galena *Gazette*, and it was published substantially as above. Judge of my surprise when a few days later Josephus Metcalf walked into my office, apparently a better man than he had been at any time since his death at Chickamauga. It seems that Metcalf had taken an overdose of the strychnine, and that the placing of his body upon an old mineral wagon to haul it over the rough roads of that country had been the salvation of him; the jolting turned his stomach, and vomiting saved him.

The best of the story remains. There is no doubt but the bullet wound of the head had affected the brain of Metcalf, thereby causing his erratic course for six or eight years, and the overdose of strychnine, giving him such a terrible shock, restored the brain to its normal condition, as he has developed no eccentricities from that time to this, fully twenty years or more. It is sufficient to say, that so far as I know, Joseph Metcalf, who has thrice been published as dead, and has as often attempted suicide, is now living, sound of mind and in fair bodily health.

Do you wonder that I can understand the case of poor Newby, and that I sadly sympathize with him in his affliction, and am ready to contribute my mite to his defense?

Yours truly,
J. C. SMITH.

The following is an extract from an article recently published in the Fairfield *Republican:*

"A PARALLEL CASE.

"The prosecution depends much on the sworn statement of the detailed soldiers that they did bury William Newby on the 8th of April, after he was shot on the 6th. Allow us to illustrate by the case of one of our own townsmen, who, as everyone knows, and would swear, is alive and with us to-day. It will probably be a surprise to many of our citizens to learn at this late day that G. J. George was slain in battle and buried on Kenesaw Mountain the same time Slow Barnhill was killed. After that battle Rev. R. H. Massey wrote home to the parents of Jasper how he was wounded, how he died, and how he was buried. The good old Methodist preacher, John Thatcher, of blessed memory, was engaged to preach the funeral. Two weeks' time was given him to think of all the good things 'Jas' had done. The day came, and with it the largest congregation that had ever met in the old Methodist church. Front seats were reserved for a host of relatives and mourners, the congregation sang 'Nearer, my God, to Thee,' the old minister took his text, 'Man that is born of woman is of few days and full of trouble,' in which he assured the bereaved parents that, inasmuch as their boy had died killing rebels, that he had gone straight to Abraham's bosom.

"It is quite certain that he made 'Jas's' case fit an angel better than those Tennesseeans can make William Newby's case fit Dan Benton.

"The citizens, thinking that not enough had been done for the memory of so good a man, called a meeting at the court-house, and long speeches were made. A committee, composed of Hon. William H. Robinson, J. W. Barnhill, both of whom are now dead, and Mr. H. H. Beecher, now of Springfield, was appointed to draft resolutions, and to set forth the many virtues that Bro. Thatcher had left out; and they wrote a clincher. The evidence of his death was just as conclusive, and, until the following October, the thing was as implicitly believed as was the story of Newby; but a man who would assert that Mr. George was buried on Kenesaw Mountain would be set down as a fool."

The facts in the case were these: On the morning of the 27th of June, 1864, I was detailed to command Company I, 40th Illinois, in the charge of Kenesaw Mountain in Georgia. We had charged to within fifty or sixty feet of the top of the mountain, where the enemy were lodged behind large piles of stone. It seemed we could go no further, so we halted. The Colonel said, "Go ahead," and we instantly uncovered and started. Barnhill and other officers, with myself, were close together. In a moment Barnhill was killed, Captain Fields was wounded, and I received a bullet wound in my right leg. I looked up, and a fellow was drawing on me with his pistol. We exchanged shots, and both missed. The next shot I struck his elbow, and he shot me in the left side, the bullet ranging down through the thigh. In ten minutes our troops fell back, and I was left lying on the top of the mountain. In one hour more I was carried away into the South.

The lieutenant who shot me took away my nice new sword, but eight days after, he died, near me in the Atlanta hospital, of lockjaw, produced by the wound he received in our encounter on the mountain.

The enemy did not bury our dead, but left

them where they had fallen, and this duty was performed by our boys the *third day*, when the enemy had evacuated the mountain. The boys wrote home that they had buried me; that they had marked the spot, and that "I died close to the enemy's works, went down fighting," etc.

From the chaplain's letter and other original papers in my possession it is plain that my death was an accepted fact until the receipt of a letter from me some months after. This letter was smuggled through the lines by being placed in the lining of the cap of Lieut. Watson, of Bangor, Me., whom I assisted to escape, and who mailed it at Knoxville, Tenn.

I wish to call attention to the significance of scars as a means of identity. Our dead had lain three days, and were very much discolored. I have a scar on my right arm caused by a cut with a knife, known, of course, to my mother. A man, who also knew of this scar, came up while they were discussing my identity, and said, "Look for a scar on his right arm." They pulled up the sleeve of the man, and no scar was visible. "It's not he," says the man. "I saw a scar on his arm when I worked for his father." He afterwards wrote to my mother that he did not bury me as the scar was not found. "Scars do not discolor until decomposition has done its complete work." The fact that this scar was not found led my mother to doubt the story of my burial, greatly mitigated her grief on the occasion of my funeral, and caused her to leave the door unlocked until my return.

How various are the fortunes of war!

I was not wounded in the head, and what sense I had, remained. It assisted me often in securing the softest plank attainable to lie upon, and in obtaining, by hook or crook, an extra meal now and then, and it also enabled me to find my way home when the war was over.

Not so poor old Newby. He was struck on the head, with brain injured and his reason destroyed. He burrowed in his hole, or wallowed in the mud at Andersonville, wandered thirty years an outcast, found his home by accident, and now looks out of jail upon a busy world full of free people, and a united country, in the saving of which he lost more than life. Why? For asking that country to take care of him during his few remaining years.

"CRAZY JACK," IN PRISON AT ANDERSONVILLE.

CHAPTER VI.

CRAZY JACK.

A PERSONALITY which injects itself into this narrative, and which makes "confusion worse confounded," is "Crazy Jack," the prisoner in Andersonville.

When the strange facts concerning the return of William Newby were sent broadcast over the land by the press of Illinois and adjoining states, and by the *National Tribune*, of Washington City, the attention of old soldiers was quickly attracted to the case.

As the nicknames and aliases appeared which had been assumed by, or thrust upon, Newby, they revived old recollections in the minds of old soldiers in different parts of the country. When the name "Crazy Jack" appeared it conjured up an ugly ghost in the remembrance of many persons who were prisoners in Andersonville in 1864-5, and they hastened to make particular inquiry, and to put themselves in evidence to the fact that they knew a creature who went by that name in Andersonville, and that he was conspicuous as being the most pitiable object in that wretched hole. At the late trial the identification was complete.

Although but six witnesses were called to the stand on this point, yet the evidence they gave was as convincing as that of the thirty Tennesseeans who swore that the prisoner was "Rickety Dan," or that of the one hundred and forty who swore that he is William Newby.

How important this identification is to our contention will appear from the following facts:

1. William Newby states that he was a soldier, was wounded at Shiloh, and sent first to Belle Isle and then to Andersonville.

2. He stated at different times and places—once in Indiana as early as 1869, that he had gone by various names, and that he was known as "Crazy Jack" at Andersonville.

3. He so represented the case to the agent of the government. He claimed all along that he was there, and we believe he was there.

Now as to "Rickety Dan":

1. He was never in the war, being too young to enlist in the U. S. army.

2. He could never have enlisted, by reason of his being rickety from birth ("wobbly," as one gentleman stated it).

3. Such was the direct evidence of those who swore that the prisoner was "Rickety Dan."

If he never was a U. S. soldier, he was never a prisoner in Andersonville.

Newby was a U. S. soldier, and the man we claim to be Newby certainly was there. These six witnesses to the fact were men whose characters or motives were never called in question. They volunteered their evidence because they conceived it to be simple justice to a most unfortunate man; a man whom they had known under the most deplorable circumstances; a man whose abject misery they had commiserated even when they themselves were suffering the nameless horrors of imprisonment. It is the experience of these men, and it is the experience of every man that languished in a southern prison, that impressions made under circumstances like these are seared as with a hot iron, and make scars that time will not efface.

I myself was a prisoner in the South six months, wounded and half starved, and I know that the impressions made there are a part of my being as I write this sentence. I say, with reverence, that I do not believe that the impressions made on the minds of the disciples at the crucifixion of Christ our Savior were more lasting.

Mr. William Snyder, of Parkersburg P. O., Richland County, Ill., testified that he belonged to the 14th Illinois Cavalry, and was captured on the Stoneman raid, July 27, 1864, near Macon, Georgia, and taken to Andersonville, and remained there three months. He says "Crazy Jack" occupied a hole in the sand-bank about thirty or forty feet from the old tent under which he took shelter. The bank was about thirty or forty feet from the channel of the creek, and was a mixture of sand and clay. This bank was about four feet high, and into it many of the unfortunate prisoners burrowed to protect themselves from the heat of the day, or the inclemency of the night. This way of "entering land" by scratching out a hole in the bank and going into it was peculiar to Andersonville. As to whether "Crazy Jack" pre-empted his claim or "jumped" it, it is idle to inquire. The chances are that it had been the property of some poor fellow who had fallen a victim to starvation and the ravages of vermin, and when Jack found it vacant he went in and possessed it. Mr. Snyder says that he saw "Crazy Jack" often, and had seen prisoners pull him out of the creek many times, where he had resorted to wash the vermin from his body and the worms from the sores on his legs. These sores he describes as loathsome, and the evidence of them remains to this day. He also says that he saw a scar on the left side of "Crazy Jack's" head, upon a certain occasion when a band of Christian people came in and shaved his hair and dressed him up in a long shirt. Upon cross-examination, Mr. Snyder was required to account for nearly every day and every act of his life. He astonished the Honorable Judge and the counsel on both sides by his accurate knowledge of the events of the war, his unusual precision in stating the sequence of events, and his connection with them. After passing successfully through this great test of memory, pointing toward the prisoner at the bar, he exclaimed, "That man is 'Crazy Jack.' I could tell him in any part of the world."

When asked by Hon. William E. Shutt, U. S. Attorney, if he positively asserted that the impressions that the claimant was "Crazy Jack," known by him in Andersonville, had never left him during the years that have intervened, and if he could see "Crazy Jack" in the person of the claimant, his answer was: "The impressions made upon the mind of a sane man under the conditions surrounding us at Andersonville remain fixed as long as life remains."

Andrew Berry, also of the 14th Illinois Cavalry, from near Carmi, Ill., was captured with Snyder. He is an intelligent man and a good citizen. He was in a different part of the prison from Mr. Snyder, but visited him often, and saw "Crazy Jack" often, and knows positively that the prisoner is the same person.

Mr. Joseph A. Russell, of the 48th Illinois Infantry, went to Andersonville about May 27, 1864. He says that he saw the prisoner walking alone on the streets of Carmi soon after he was brought home by his son, Ki Newby, and recognized him at once as "Crazy Jack" of Andersonville, and he could not be mistaken.

Mr. H. J. Jamison, of White County, was taken to Andersonville in the spring of 1864. He belonged to the 56th Illinois Infantry, and saw "Crazy Jack" there. He had the scurvy very bad, and did not have sense enough to keep out of the dirty water. There could be no mistake about its being "Jack."

Joseph Downey, of New Haven, Ill., was a prisoner in Andersonville eleven months. Mr.

CRAZY JACK. 85

Downey is a bright, intelligent man, and says that he often saw the prisoner at Andersonville, and that he was called "Crazy Jack."

Mr. Uriah King is a resident of Sangamon County, Ill., and was a member of the 24th Illinois Infantry, and described the hole occupied by "Crazy Jack" as a dug-out in the bank of the creek. He says that he saw him when his hair was cut, but did not see the scar on his head. He says that "Crazy Jack" and the prisoner are one and the same person, and that there can be no doubt about it.

Letters have been received by the writer and the attorneys from remote parts of the country stating that they knew "Crazy Jack" in Andersonville, describing him as above, at least three of them mentioning the particular hole into which he crawled, and giving its precise location.

A letter has just been handed me, addressed to N. E. Roberts, editor of the Fairfield *Republican*. It was written by Captain Isham M. Blake, of Lloyd, Jefferson County, Florida, under date of August 13, 1893, in which he says, "I was an officer in the Confederate army, and knew one federal soldier in an Illinois regiment by the name of William Newby confined in the stockade at Andersonville." His attention was called to the name by the Chicago *Inter-Ocean*, and he refers to Senators Call and Pasco.

Whatever else may be settled or left unsettled in the mind of the reader, he must conclude that these witnesses saw "Crazy Jack" at Andersonville, and that they see him in the person of the prisoner. It is clear, also, that whether the prisoner be William Newby of Illinois or Dan Benton of Tennessee, he is "Crazy Jack" of Andersonville.

AN OUTLINE OF THE LIFE OF THE PRISONER, WHO
DANIEL BENTON, AND WHOM THE DEFENSE CI

SEPARATE HISTORY.

WILLIAM NEWBY.

Born in Tennessee in the year......... 1826
Moved to Illinois in the year.......................... 1832
His father died about the year........................... 1840
                1844...........
Marries Ferebe Files in the year....... .... 1849..... .....
                1851
                to
                1858...........
                1858
                to
William Newby enlists in army...... ....1861...........
William Newby wounded at Shiloh......................1862...........

         AT THIS POINT THE TWO LIVES
              1864
Prisoner in Andersonville known as "Crazy Jack".......1865....Prisone
         FROM THIS POINT THEY RUN INTO
              1868.
Prisoner in Pike County poorhouse, under name of Allen Lewis, states
    Granny White Pike in Tennessee with two women an

          1869, 1870, 1871, 1872, 1873, :
Prisoner making the rounds of the poorhouses in Pike and Greene coun
    Peter Fair that he was a Union soldier and was shot at Shil
       in Andersonville; that he was called Bill

              1877.
Arrested in Camden, Tenn., for stealing a horse and sentenced to the p
           alias Dan Benton.

              1879.
  Escapes from prison and surrendered to the officers by Lydia

              1889.
      Is released, and finds his way to the Indian.

              1890.
Finds his way into Illinois, where he is recognized and restored to h
          applied for discharge.

              1893.
Goes with the government agent to Tennessee, and evidence procured tl
    indicted, tried, and found guilty of attempting to perpeti
      by falsely representing himself to be \

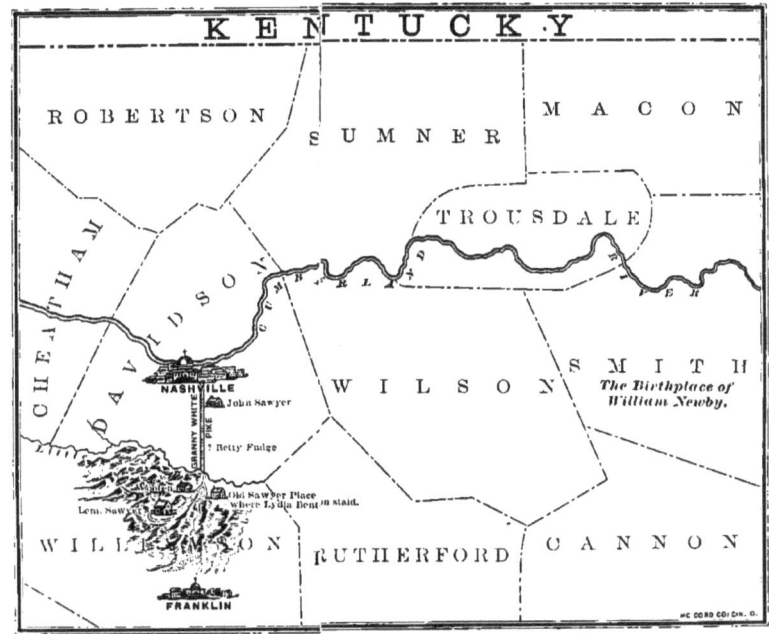

SKETCH OF PART OF TENNESSEE AROUND NASHVILLE, SHOWING "GRANNY WHITE PIKE" AND SAWYER SETTLEMENT, ALSO SMITH COUNTY, THE BIRTHPLACE OF WILLIAM NEWBY.

M THE PROSECUTION CLAIMS TO BE
AIMS TO BE WILLIAM NEWBY.

DANIEL BENTON.

..............Benton born in White County, Ill.
................Benton is taken to Tennessee.
................Benton lives with the Sawyers.
................Benton generally in poorhouse.
.... Benton wounded by wagon-bow.
CONFLICT.

r seen in Tenn. and recognized as "Rickety Dan."
ONE HISTORY.

then that he was shot at Shiloh. Was seen on
d recognized as Daniel Benton.
1874.
ties under the name of Daniel Benton. Relates to
oh; that he was called "Crazy Jack"
Newby in Illinois.

enitentiary for sixteen years. Name, Allen Lewis,

Benton, for which she received $12.50.

poorhouses again.

is family. Applied for pension, having previously

at he is the son of Lydia Benton. Brought back,
ate a fraud upon the government
illiam Newby.

CHAPTER VII.

DAN BENTON.

ABOUT the year 1843 or 1844, when William Newby, then a stout boy seventeen years of age, was working on his mother's farm in White County, there was born, in a remote part of the same county, the child that was to have such a malign influence upon the destiny of the unsuspecting young farmer.

This child, the offspring of an erring girl, came into the world without the sanction of the law, and was the natural heir to a rich heritage of poverty, sorrow, and suffering. Besides the misfortunes which are the usual birthright of his kind, from the time of his unwelcome advent into the world he was afflicted with the rickets, a disease of bone and limb that makes locomotion difficult to perform and painful to observe.

His mother, Lydia Benton, became a servant and dependent in the house of Nicholas Pyle,

AN OUTLINE OF THE LIFE OF THE PRISONER, WHOM THE PROSECUTION CLAIMS TO BE DANIEL BENTON, AND WHOM THE DEFENSE CLAIMS TO BE WILLIAM NEWBY.

SEPARATE HISTORY.

WILLIAM NEWBY.		DANIEL BENTON.
Born in Tennessee in the year.........................1826		
Moved to Illinois in the year.........................1832		
His father died about the year.........................1840		
	1844............................Benton born in White County, Ill.	
Marries Ferebe Files in the year.....................1849............................Benton is taken to Tennessee.		
	1851 to 1858............................Benton lives with the Sawyers.	
	1858 to	
William Newby enlists in army........................1861............................Benton generally in poorhouse.		
William Newby wounded at Shiloh....................1862............................Benton wounded by wagon-bow.		

AT THIS POINT THE TWO LIVES CONFLICT.

1864

Prisoner in Andersonville known as "Crazy Jack".......1865....Prisoner seen in Tenn. and recognized as "Rickety Dan."

FROM THIS POINT THEY RUN INTO ONE HISTORY.

1868.

Prisoner in Pike County poorhouse, under name of Allen Lewis, states then that he was shot at Shiloh. Was seen on Granny White Pike in Tennessee with two women and recognized as Daniel Benton.

1869, 1870, 1871, 1872, 1873, 1874.

Prisoner making the rounds of the poorhouses in Pike and Greene counties under the name of Daniel Benton. Relates to Peter Fair that he was a Union soldier and was shot at Shiloh; that he was called "Crazy Jack" in Andersonville; that he was called Bill Newby in Illinois.

1877.

Arrested in Camden, Tenn., for stealing a horse and sentenced to the penitentiary for sixteen years. Name, Allen Lewis, alias Dan Benton.

1879.

Escapes from prison and surrendered to the officers by Lydia Benton, for which she received $12.50.

1889.

Is released, and finds his way to the Indiana poorhouses again.

1890.

Finds his way into Illinois, where he is recognized and restored to his family. Applied for pension, having previously applied for discharge.

1893.

Goes with the government agent to Tennessee, and evidence procured that he is the son of Lydia Benton. Brought back, indicted, tried, and found guilty of attempting to perpetrate a fraud upon the government by falsely representing himself to be William Newby.

who kindly sheltered the unfortunates, and here Dan existed rather than lived, and, like Topsy, "growed" in the absence of what mothers call "raising."

Many old people who lived in that neighborhood, among whom are two of the Pyle family, remember the child and his mother during the period between 1846 and 1850. They remember him as being a little cripple, and some mention that he was especially affected in the right leg, and Mrs. Acord, a woman of fifty-five years of age, remembers well that her father, Nicholas Pyle, constructed a "walking-horse," a contrivance to assist the child in learning to walk. By the rule which usually governs the naming of illegitimate children he received for his "blood" name that of his mother, Benton; for his christian, or "water," name, for less obvious reasons, that of Daniel. Henceforth he was known as Daniel Benton.

He is described as being of light complexion, blue eyes, light hair, somewhat sunken between the eyes, this last peculiarity producing an effect upon the countenance which caused him to be variously described as "snub" or pug-nosed. Two of the members of Nicholas Pyle's family state upon oath that the boy Daniel Benton was again in that neighborhood in the year 1863, and was still of light complexion and blue eyes. In the year 1849 or 1850 one Andrew Wooten, a hillside farmer from Tennessee, whose two-years' stay in Illinois had brought neither wealth nor contentment, loaded up his cart, and taking Lydia Benton and Dan, who was then about six years old, under his protection, headed his steers for his old haunts on the banks of the Little Harper.

As this vicinity is to be the future home of Dan, and the scene of his many mysterious appearances and disappearances, I may as well describe the locality in this place as in any other.

From Nashville, the capital of Tennessee, running southwardly through a rich, undulating country, is a highway known as the Granny White Pike. Ten or twelve miles south of Nashville it strikes a creek know as the Little Harper, the southern boundary of Davidson County, and the northern boundary of Williamson, the county seat of which is Franklin.

South of the creek the roads among the hills separate, and worm by tortuous courses on toward the south. On the benches, spurs, hillsides, backbones of ridges, and in the heads of hollows, and fringed along the roadsides, is the aggregation of houses known as the Sawyer Settlement.

Settlements on the barren hillsides contiguous to small streams need not be particularly described, as the characteristics of the people composing them are the same in every state. One-story, round-log houses as a rule, with now and then one more pretentious, having two stories, but devoid of "piazzas," and neither "chinked" nor "daubed"; little pole stables; draw-bars for gates; a four-rail fence to prevent the children from rolling down the hill; little patches of corn on the hillside or in the bottom, with a sufficient number of hounds to fence them, is a description applying with more or less accuracy to all.

The people are kind-hearted, well-meaning, and hospitable, and contented to a fault. They manage to live well. If spareribs and porterhouse run short, are there not the woods and the creek hard by? One member of the family is detailed to bring in a string of fish, and another to knock down a squirrel, or to pick up a terrapin, and peace and plenty reign in that household. I am speaking of this class of hill and hollow-dwellers in general, and as they are found all over the country. There are, I am told, some good small farmers on Granny White Pike, after you strike the hills. I will mention it, not by way of reflection, but as an instance of their great, good fortune, that some farmers who came as witnesses for the government against Newby probably realized more hard cash from this job than they have from their farms for the last three years.

From the evidence of the Tennessee people we learn that Dan arrived there on time, and shortly after took up his abode with a family by the name of Sawyer, with whom he lived several years. Little can be learned as to Dan's personal appearance from these people, except that "he looked then as he does now." As to Dan's mental caliber at this period, the weight of testimony goes to show that he was sound in mind, and of remarkably good memory. His crippled condition developed a gait which, it seems, must have resembled that of Newby, and can not, therefore, be easily described. One gentleman, in attempting to describe it, said that he walked as though at every step he would fall on his head. Mrs. Betty Fudge, who was a Sawyer, and claimed great familiarity with Dan as a playmate, describes him as teetering around in dresses when eight or nine years old, a fact which is suggestive of a peculiar custom of the neighborhood, or an abnormal condition of the boy's physical structure.

Many testify to playing with Dan when a boy. One gentleman recalls the fact that he once hit him on the head with a brick, from which it may be inferred that Dan took a passive rather than an active part in the amusements. Old man Wooten, who, it seems, continued to take an interest in the boy, winds up his antebellum history in the statement that he put Dan in the poorhouse a few years before the war, where he probably remained most of the time until the war broke out.

We are indebted, however, to the recollection of four gentlemen, three of the Alleys and a Mr. Holley, for the only definite circumstance connected with Dan's life that can be angled out of the history of those years. They remember that about the beginning of the war, probably very near the time that Newby was shot at Shiloh, Dan was standing around, boy-like, in the way, where some men were bending a wagon-bow. The bow kicked out and struck Dan on the left side of the head above the ear, precisely where Newby was shot. They stated that the doctor sewed up the wound, and the boy continued to "wobble" as usual.

This is the unvarnished history, so far as it can be traced, of the boy whose name, bodily deformity, and "heritage of sorrows" was to be fastened on, and become a part of the history of, William Newby.

Both are now brought to the year of 1862, and to the state of Tennessee.

Think of Tennessee in 1862. Think how the fearful cyclone of war swept over that state, and of the armies that surged back and forth through Nashville, and over the Granny White Pike. Down poured the rebels after the capture of Donaldson, to reach their new base of defense at Corinth. Down came the Federals on their way to support Grant's army at Shiloh. Back came Buell's army to oppose the movements of Bragg; and when that invasion was over, both armies were massed in the neighborhood, where, not long after, the thunder of cannons at Murpheysboro, a few miles away, made those old hills tremble to their bases.

Where was poor Dan then?

Like William Newby, he was swallowed up in the vortex of war.

As stated before, two living members of the family of Nicholas Pyle, the man who kept Dan and his mother until he was six years old, state upon oath that Dan came back to the old place in White County in 1863. From this we will have to infer that when the war broke loose in its fury, he "took to the open country like a frightened rat from a barn on fire," and sought the more peaceful atmosphere of Illinois. Many believe that Dan now fills an unknown grave, and that some unknown man fills the grave of Newby, but, be they alive or be they dead, from this point, one and inseparable, their lives "go marching on."

It has always seemed a sort of poetic injustice that the clear and lovely Mississippi should lose its identity, and that its distinctive loveliness should be buried in the muddy waters of the Missouri. No less pity is it that the grand old Missouri, after moving majestically through the continent in its sweep from the far-off Rockies, should all at once be robbed of its name, and that its grand volume should contribute to the name and fame of one of its own tributaries.

As one looks into the waters of these two rivers as they mingle in their lower course he seems to detect a spirit of unrest and mutual discontent as they flow together in sullen silence to the sea.

That two human lives should become so

merged into each other as to cover up the identity of both; that the web and woof should become so tangled as to baffle every effort to pick out a single thread belonging exclusively to either, is a stranger and a sadder thing.

Yet such has been the melancholy fate of the prisoner.

Some idea may be gathered of the confusion and perplexity connected with the question of this man's identity by a glance at the condition of affairs in the court-room during the late trial. Before you you have the prisoner, a large, swarthy, black-haired, dark-eyed man, whose likeness you have in these pages. The dazed expression of his countenance, the rolling of his eyes, and his rambling, incoherent talk, indicate an unbalanced mind. His height, length of limb, and strong muscles of the back are suggestive of a once powerful man. The jerking and twitching of the head, the dangling arms, the gait, half shuffle and half lunge, indicate a loss of control over what are known as the voluntary muscles of the body. On his head and body are several scars. He says his name is William Newby.

In the court-room is an array of witnesses, some two hundred and fifty in all, and from three states in the Union, gathered to decide who this prisoner of the government may be. The contention is: Is the man at the bar the mental and physical wreck of William Newby, who, at the age of thirty-six, was shot in the head at Shiloh, or is he the natural development of Daniel Benton, the fair-complected, blue-eyed, "rickety" boy, of sound mind, who, at the age of sixteen, was wounded on the head by the wagon-bow, the same year, on the Granny White Pike.

First comes a gray-haired woman, more than sixty years of age, and says: "The man is my husband, William Newby, whom I married forty-four years ago. He is the man who kissed me and our six children when he started for the war thirty-two years ago. I know it to be him by his face and features, still familiar, though marked by time and suffering. I know him by the deep knowledge that twelve years of mutual love, with all the cares and labors of building our home and raising our children, would beget. I know him by the marks and scars on his person. I know him by the mutual knowledge of the sacred, secret inner life that only husband and wife may know."

The man is William Newby.

One hundred and forty of the old friends, neighbors, and comrades of her husband, looking at the prisoner at the bar, say: "The man is William Newby."

Then comes an old veteran, who says: "I know this man. I knew him in Andersonville prison. I was acquainted with him in 1864, under circumstances that would preclude the possibility of my being mistaken as long as life and reason remain with me. The man's name is 'Crazy Jack.'"

And six other old prisoners from Andersonville examine the prisoner at the bar and say: "This is Crazy Jack."

Then come more than thirty people from the state of Tennessee, who say: "This man we have known from our youth up. His mother dwelt among us, and we have played with him a thousand times. We can not be mistaken. He walks now as he did then, and looks now as he did then. We are used to seeing his familiar but ungainly form passing up and down the Granny White Pike. Some of us saw him in 1864. Many of us saw him in 1868. We have known him in poorhouses and we have known him in prison. As sure as there is a God in Heaven, the prisoner at the bar is none other than 'Rickety Dan' Benton, of Tennessee."

A scene like this would almost justify the conclusion on the part of the prisoner himself that "all men are liars," or that the rest of the world had gone crazy.

Since nothing can be gathered from the opinions of the witnesses, the inquirer turns to the evidence in the case. When he has carefully considered the proven or admitted facts, the following are some of the difficulties that will confront him:

If the prisoner be William Newby, how does it happen that since the year 1870 he has adopted and worn the name Daniel Benton?

If he be William Newby, how did it happen that when Dan Benton disappeared, that he was known in the neighborhood as Dan Benton? Acknowledged Lydia Benton as his mother, and was acknowledged by her as her son?

If he be William Newby, how could the thirty Tennesseeans mistake him for Dan Benton, whom they claim to have seen, at intervals, from his boyhood to the year 1889?

On the other hand, if he be Dan Benton, how does it happen that he has five or six distinct marks and scars on his person corresponding exactly to those known to have been on the person of Newby before the war?

If he be Dan Benton, how could he have been

in Andersonville as Crazy Jack at the same time he, a boy of twenty, was passing up and down the Pike in Tennessee?

If he be Dan Benton, how did he happen many years ago to tell Peter Fair, the government witness, from the Pike County poorhouse, that he had been wounded in the battle of Shiloh; that he had been a prisoner in Andersonville, and that he was known there as Crazy Jack; and that he was known in Illinois as William Newby?

If he be Dan Benton, how comes he to be familiar with events, places, roads, localities, old landmarks, improvements which Dan Benton never, by any possibility, could have heard of, and many of which had passed into the region of the forgotten until recalled by the prisoner himself in his lucid moments?

The history of Dan Benton as a distinct individual having come to an abrupt termination with the beginning of the war, and having given the reader some idea of the complications growing out of the subsequent history, I can do no better than to chronicle the facts relating to the acts and wanderings of the prisoner, which one side claims to be those of Daniel Benton, the other side those of William Newby.

The first time the two characters came in conflict after their simultaneous disappearance was in 1864–5.

We have seen heretofore how the prisoner was seen and known in Andersonville under the name of Crazy Jack, and thought by the witnesses to be about thirty-five or thirty-eight years of age.

Now comes Washington Bond, of Tennessee, and states that at this identical time he met Dan Benton, now the prisoner, one mile from Hillsboro, wearing a dark suit of clothes, and riding a mare. He said to the prisoner, "How are you, Dan?" and he said, "How are you, Wash?"

Richard M. Daniel had a farm, but lived with Lydia Benton in 1865, and Dan came there and stole his horse in daylight. It developed later on that he never paid for it himself, it probably being an old relic of Bragg's invasion, or a remnant of Hood's army, which collapsed a few miles from there late in 1864.

J. W. Alley saw him in 1864, and knows, moreover, that Dan got his head hurt after the war, as he was present at the time. T. J. Burnham saw him on the Pike at the close of the war. Robert H. Hill said that he saw him in 1864 or 1865.

From the evidence of these two sets of witnesses we have on the one hand the boy Dan developing into a young fellow of twenty, lawless, mean, and rickety, dressed up, and having a love for riding; on the other hand we have a man of thirty-eight, naked, demented, being dragged out of the mud. It is easy to conceive that both characters are true and real, but the difficulty is, the seven men on the one hand and the five men on the other swear to the fact that the prisoner before them is the man whom they saw.

Three years more go by, and we come to the year 1868. Peter Fair, an inmate of the Pike County, Ind., poorhouse, a witness brought by the government, stated that he knew the prisoner well, and had seen him often.

For many years it had been the habit of the prisoner to make the circuit of the poorhouses of southern Indiana. He had drifted into the Pike County poorhouse in 1868, and enrolled himself as Allen Lewis. Since that time he had come and gone often. His return has been periodic. In his peripatetic wanderings he has seen him come and go with less regularity, but with the certainty of the wild goose. He has learned to gaze on his wobbling gait as it carried him into the dim perspective, and to confidently expect his return.

In the year 1868 the prisoner was seen by as many as a dozen of the witnesses on the Granny White Pike in company with two women. Betty Fudge, the playmate and companion of his youthful days, testified that Daniel halted in front of her gate on the Pike, and one of the women asked for a melon that was in sight; that Dan stood at the gate, and that she never spoke to him. Several saw him, and knew him by his rickety walk, but few spoke to him. Those who did, state that he was inquiring the way to Lydia Benton's. The dozen witnesses who saw him on this trip with the women all swear that it was in the year 1868, and it was the opinion of every one of them that he was about thirty years old at that time. These people testified that Dan was about thirteen to fifteen at the beginning of the war, and he could not have been, according to their own testimony, over twenty-two or twenty-three at the time they say they saw him on the Pike.

Another singular circumstance connected with that trip is the fact that those who spoke to him say that he was manifesting a desire to get to the home of his alleged mother, Lydia Benton, and, although within a mile or two of the place, there is no evidence that he ever went there at that time. The woman with whom he traveled on the Pike in 1873 or 1874, and who was the woman, evidently, who stopped at Betty Fudge's, states that they never went to see Lydia Benton, and that she never saw her in her life.

Whether those people were right or wrong in regard to the prisoner being there in 1868, we find him at one of his favorite poorhouses in Green County, Ind., in 1869. Pike and Green County poorhouses are about fifty miles apart, and while on his circuit he registered at these two at the following times: Green, in 1869; Pike, 1870; and again Pike in 1872; Green, in 1873, 1874, and 1875; his stay at these resorts varying from a few weeks to a much longer period.

In 1872, in the Pike County poorhouse, his connection with Hannah Stewart begins. Peter Fair states that at about this time they left the poorhouse together. She herself says, "My child by Stewart was born in 1872, and in the spring we left the poorhouse, and in about a year we, together with another woman, were on the Granny White Pike, in Williamson County, Tenn."

Under this common-law marriage the prisoner and Hannah lived and moved and starved together for years as they went their weary rounds. There is no evidence that either was not as faithful to their self-imposed vows as those who march to the altar to the sound of the organ, whose vows are solemnized by priest or preacher under wreaths of orange-blossoms. Two children was the result of this attachment, one of whom died, and the other, a half-witted boy of sixteen, lives in Tennessee with his mother.

In 1877 the prisoner, who had wandered to Benton County, on the Tennessee River, was arrested for stealing a horse. Court was in session at Camden, the county-seat at the time. The next day the prisoner was indicted by the grand jury, and taken before the court, plead guilty, sentenced for a term of sixteen years in the penitentiary, and the third day was shipped to Nashville to serve out his term.

There is little information to be had on this matter except the record itself, which shows the facts as above related. The prisoner, of course, can give no coherent account of the affair. The general tenor of his story is that he tired of walking, and concluded that he would ride a while for a change, and when ready to do so he intended to turn the horse loose. He was caught, taken back to Camden, and sentenced. It is likely that horse-stealing was too prevalent in the vicinity at that time, and a good victim was wanted. It is pretty certain that no investigation was made as to the mental condition of the man. That he was crazy, as he now is, only to a greater degree, is plain from this fact: When he was sent to Nashville to the penitentiary he soon became a "trusty," that is, trusted to go beyond the walls of the prison to do errands or to perform labor outside. It had been the prisoner's privilege to drive up the cows for the warden. After he had been there for two years, he became weary of the restraint, and one day, when sent by the warden to drive up his cow, he procured a suit of citizen's clothes, hid under a culvert to put them on, and walked off down the Granny White Pike until he struck the hills, and halted in the Sawyer neighborhood. In a day or two he was caught, the Sawyers say, at Lydia Benton's, who, they say, gave him up for half the reward, or $12.50.

By running away this time he forfeited all his "good time," by which is meant the amount of time deducted from the length of his term for good conduct. The trustees, after he was taken back, restored his good time, "because he was of feeble mind and a cripple." This is the language of the record. It is very evident, then, that he was of "feeble mind and a cripple" when he was put in the penitentiary, and had been for years. There is abundant proof that the prisoner was feeble-minded from the statements of the government's witnesses. Dr. Mayfield examined him, and found him to be of feeble mind. Another witness speaks of him being a trusty, wheeling dirt on the outside, and still another relates that while he was working in the penitentiary the prisoner knew enough to open gates when people instructed him to do so.

If, then, he was in that condition when he stole the horse, we can easily understand why little is known besides the bare record. He was marched to the court-house in Camden, and asked if he took the horse. He said, "I did." "Sixteen years in the penitentiary." The whole thing was done in less time, and attracted less attention, than an ordinary three-dollar case before a justice of the peace.

There is something peculiar in this Lydia Benton matter. We have just seen how she turned the prisoner over to the authorities for the $12.50 reward; we have noted that when he and the women were on the Pike in 1868, as the people there claim, or in 1874, as the woman herself claims, that he did not go to the house of Lydia; and it is another singular fact that during the time he was in the penitentiary he was never heard or known to have called her his mother—always Lydia Benton. It will not do to say that the whole "Mother Lydia Benton" story is a fabrication, any more than it will do to say that a whole community in Illinois are telling what they know to be false when they relate the story of Newby's recollection of events long past. But there are internal evidences in these stories of the prisoner's relation to this woman that forces the conviction that there is a great mistake somewhere, and whatever that relation was, and wherever it may have begun, she knew that he was not her son, and he knew that she was not his mother.

There is one characteristic running through the history of this prisoner that would seem to show that it was Newby and not Dan Benton. We know from abundant testimony that Newby was shot in the head, and very badly wounded. Thousands of examples attest the fact that such wounds are liable to affect the brain in such a manner as to destroy the reason, and to paralyze the members of the body. When the prisoner was in Andersonville, whither he had been moved from Belle Isle, we find him helpless—both crippled and demented. All along the line he is accredited by those that met him with little sense. His good time was restored to him in the prison on account of being feeble-minded. That was in 1889. Those who have read of his return in 1890 will see at once that he was not of sound mind. To-day it is perfectly plain to everybody that his mind, though greatly improved in the last two years, is yet far from sound.

Notwithstanding the testimony of the witnesses, as above stated; notwithstanding the testimony of the physician, Dr. Mayfield, and of the prison records themselves, that he was "of feeble mind and a cripple" (and for that reason he received the only kindness which those people ever bestowed on him—his "good time"), notwithstanding all this, the theory of the government is that the prisoner is a sane, shrewd, designing fraud and scoundrel.

This implies that disguised in that rickety frame is a brain to conceive, a mind to plan, and a will to execute deep-laid schemes. By this theory he is credited with powers of invention sufficient to enable him, unaided and alone, to originate a scheme for defrauding the government that would have done credit to the genius of Aaron Burr. According to this theory, he was not crazy, as the prison authorities supposed, but his "feeble-mindedness" was only a part of his deep-laid scheme. He was cunningly laying the wires when he told in Indiana of being shot at Shiloh, and of being in Andersonville. He was simply preparing for a raid on Illinois, when he stated that he was known by the name of Newby in that state. He had never seen Newby, or been seen by him, yet he proposed to saunter into the country where Newby had formerly lived, knowing that some old soldier would drop his eye upon him, recognize him, and announce that the old soldier had returned. He came, and the plot is carried out according to the programme, and when he found himself sought after by the people he had come to delude with consummate shrewdness, he attempted to get out of the state into Indiana, knowing that he would be pursued, overtaken, and returned by anxious dupes, and compelled by deluded but well-meaning natives to apply for a pension.

The theory of the government and the verdict of the jury imply that all this nonsense is true.

It is difficult to believe that twelve men could be found to believe the one, or to subscribe to the other.

At the beginning of this chapter I started out with the design and promise of giving the reader the history of Daniel Benton. That duty I claim to have performed honestly and impartially, until the light of history grew fainter and fainter, until it shone with only a faint and dubious beam, and then went out in the darkness altogether. I then reviewed the history of the prisoner, who, as has often been stated or implied, carries with him the names and histories of both Benton and Newby, is afflicted with physical infirmities common to both, and is doubtless the living image of one or the other of those historic men. The question which of these two characters the living man represents is rendered exceedingly difficult from the fact that his own acts and deeds for the last thirty years are the accredited history of both.

When instructing the jury on this point of identification the judge made the following statement: "The resemblance of one man to another physically often misleads, but the old aphorism that 'no two men are alike within' is full of wisdom for your guidance."

It is very clear that the identity of this man can not be settled by testimony on the ground of personal resemblance, for, as we have seen, more than thirty people swear that he bears the image and likeness of Benton, and more than one hundred swear that the personal resemblance is that of Newby.

We are forced, then, as was the jury, by the necessity of the case, and by the wisdom of the aphorism, to conclude that the prisoner before us is Dan Benton, if his mental condition conforms to that of Dan Benton, or that it is Newby if mentally he most resembles Newby; or, in other words, he is the man who, compared with himself, is found, in the language of His Honor, to be "morally, socially, and mentally the same within." As to morals, both Newby and Benton have been accused of thefts. Socially, they both moved in poorhouse society, and one was the son and the other the associate of a fallen woman. Since, then, physical resemblance and moral and social characteristics fail to distinguish them, we must look into the mental conditions of the men.

For the general information of the reader and for the purposes of this comparison, the mental condition of the prisoner, ascertained by personal observation and also upon the authority of neighbors, friends, and his family physician, may be stated about as follows:

His mind is better now than when he returned. At that time he was subject to fits, but good treatment and general improvement in health has made these of very rare occurrence, and have tended to greatly restore his mind. At present, in his lucid intervals, he will talk rationally upon a subject that he knows anything about, for two to five minutes, but after that he runs wild.

On quiet days, when in good health, not worried, or embarrassed by a crowd, he frequently talks sensibly for a short time, but when out of health or annoyed he is perfectly irrational.

"At no time," says a gentleman who has observed him closely, "has his mind been in such a condition that you could sit down and talk with him right along for more than five minutes at a time."

With the mental condition of this man we will compare the mental condition of Benton, as shown by the witnesses for the prosecution.

W. K. McDowell testified that he knew Benton when a boy, and "he was never of unsound mind and never subject to fits."

Robert D. Reed: "Played with Dan when a boy. He always appeared to be of sound mind, and never subject to fits."

Mrs. Angelina Sawyer "knew Dan from the time he was six years old. When a youth he never had fits, had a sound mind, and a remarkable memory."

And so on through the list of the thirty Tennesseeans who knew the boy up to the war. The question as to Dan's mental condition was put to all, and was answered with many variations, but to the same effect by all.

He was characterized as being "smart enough," "cunning," "sharp," "cute," "smart as other people," etc. Many testified to being his constant companion and playmate, and the direct and indirect evidence is that in intellect he was the equal of any of them.

This comparison has been fairly made, and shows conclusively that there is not the least similarity between the prisoner and Dan Benton. On the other hand, it is clearly seen that in bent, strength, and condition of mind they are absolutely and entirely different.

Nor does the real Dan Benton conform any more closely to the alleged Dan Benton known after the war. This individual, as has been, and can be more fully shown by the government witnesses, was in a condition almost identical with the prisoner at the present time.

The evidence is perfectly conclusive, as has been shown before, that in the penitentiary he was considered crazy. Permit me to again refer to the fact that the records of the prison speak of their alleged Dan Benton as being "of feeble mind and a cripple." Dr. Mayfield, the assistant state physician, said, "He was not regarded by me as being mentally well balanced."

Lem Sawyer, when speaking in reference to his return to the prison, said that he did not regard Dan as being of a sound mind.

These statements, with others that have been given, and still others that could be given, go to prove that it was well known to all connected with the penitentiary that the man they claim to be Dan Benton was of unsound mind. The actions of the man himself prove it. When he escaped from the prison, if it were true that Lydia Benton was his mother, it was the act of a crazy man to go and put up at her house, only twelve miles away from the penitentiary, right under the shadows of the homes of Sawyer, Wells, and Talkington, officers of the prison.

The discovery was made by all these people

while he was in the penitentiary that he was of unsound mind, a discovery which might have been made by them when he traveled on the Granny White Pike in 1868 or 1873 had they not passed him, as they say they did, in silent contempt, or with a few words at most.

The plain facts of the case are, that the individual known after the war, and claimed to be Dan Benton, closely resembles in mental characteristics and general actions the prisoner at the bar, while neither the prisoner nor that individual has the remotest resemblance to the real Dan Benton.

The prisoner and the man known after the war by the various names are acknowledged to be one and the same person. That the prisoner is of feeble and unsound mind is a matter of observation. That the individual referred to was of feeble mind has been abundantly proved. It has also been proven that Dan Benton before the war was in this particular the opposite of both. Then these questions force themselves upon us:

When and wherefore did Dan Benton cease to have light hair, blue eyes, and light complexion, and become a swarthy, dark-haired, dark-eyed man?

When and wherefore did Daniel Benton

change from a bright and cunning youth to a man of feeble mind?

How happens it that those who profess to have known Dan all his life can give no account as to when and how these changes in his physical and mental condition occurred?

When the alleged Dan Benton was released from prison in 1889, why did he turn his steps northward, toward distant poorhouses in Indiana, instead of going to his mother's home a few miles down the Pike?

Daniel Benton is too difficult to understand. I think that an easier solution of the identity of the mysterious personage on trial may be found in William Newby.

We have seen how he was shot in the head at Shiloh, and left on the field. We have given the circumstances tending to raise a doubt as to his having been killed at the time. In addition to those already given, it will be found in the history of the trial that two of his comrades, not heretofore mentioned, went to the battlefield after the engagement and searched for the body of Newby, and failed to find it, although the bodies of the other members of the company were found.

The question as to whether he was or was not

buried on the third day, Tuesday, has been fully discussed. It may be added in this connection that the testimony of Dr. Merritt, one of the men who positively swore that they buried William Newby on Tuesday, is further weakened by the fact that he states in the evidence that "Newby was shot in the forehead, over one eye."

I think that it will be conceded that there is a strong probability that he was carried away a prisoner by the enemy. Much stranger things have happened. The man whom we are trying to identify claims that, although he has for a long period of time been called Dan Benton and various other names, he is the identical William Newby that the men above referred to sought for and failed to find, and that he was carried away prisoner, and was sent first to Belle Isle and then to Andersonville. The evidence is conclusive that this man was in Andersonville, and known as "Crazy Jack." He was demented and crippled. Learned doctors testify that an injury to the head such as Newby was known to have received would be likely to produce such results. By examining the testimony of Peter Fair it will be seen that as far back as 1868, when going by the name of Allen Lewis, he said he was shot at Shiloh ; was hurt on the head by a piece of bomb, and that it made him crazy. In 1889 he stated that he had been known as Crazy Jack, and that in Illinois he was known as Bill Newby.

The prisoner bears several marks and scars that were known to be on the person of Newby before the war, and at lucid intervals he relates facts and circumstances which could be known only to Newby himself. Why, then, is he not William Newby?

Because he has by some means acquired the name of Benton. Because it is claimed that he looks like Dan Benton. Because he is said to have frequented the neighborhood where Dan Benton lived. Because it is alleged that he and the mother of Dan Benton naturally acknowledged the relation of mother and son.

Are these facts capable of an explanation?

In regard to the question as to which individual the prisoner most resembles, I think that the description given of Dan in his childhood and the opinions of the hundred or more Illinois people may be fairly considered as a set-off against the opinions of the thirty witnesses from Tennessee.

The question as to how he chanced to wander

into the neighborhood of Nashville would be difficult to answer. It might be that an image of that dreadful scene where he was shot was photographed dimly on his mind, and this at first was all the picture of his past life that presented itself to his consciousness, and, like a murderer, he might have been drawn by some mysterious influence back toward the spot where the tragedy occurred.

Again, by looking at the map, you will discover that a straight line drawn from Andersonville prison to the home of Newby in Illinois will pass directly through Nashville. When Newby was turned out of prison he may have been shipped by some one as far as Nashville in the direction of his home.

It will also be remembered that the birthplace of William Newby was in Smith County, Tenn. By reference to the map it will be seen that this county lies very near to Nashville, and it is quite certain that Newby was born, and lived until he was six years old, within forty miles of that city. His old mother told me recently that so loth was she to leave that country that at one time, on their journey to Illinois, they turned back and journeyed three days toward their old home, but finally decided to come west. It is likely that his childish recollections and the oft-repeated stories of his mother had made impressions of his native country as vivid to his shattered mind as those of later years, and those impressions may have caused him to gravitate in that direction. Since he did not go home, he was as likely, at least, to drop into that neighborhood as into any other.

How did he receive the name Dan Benton? The transferring of names is very frequently and very easily done. It is a matter of common observation and universal experience that if, by reason of accident, an individual receives a temporary injury that causes a peculiar limp or gait, or a comical change in the expression of the face, or unnaturalness in the voice, he is jokingly called "Old So-and-So," referring to the man (or cow, for that matter) that suggests the comparison.

We are told that Dan Benton had the same rickety walk that the prisoner has. He was remarked and noticed in the surrounding country, and up and down the pike, by reason of his "wobbling" gait. He was in Nashville often, and, according to the statement of one gentleman, he walked from the poorhouse to Franklin nearly every Saturday. He was also known in surrounding towns. Two or three armies were stationed in the neighborhood at different times. "Rickety Dan" was a frequenter of camps, and was employed by the soldiers to smuggle whisky. It is reasonable to suppose, then, that many people were acquainted with the name and walk of "Rickety Dan." The weight of evidence shows that at the beginning of the war, say 1862, the real Dan disappeared from the immediate neighborhood, and was not seen there again until 1868. Indeed, the age the witnesses place upon the man they claim to have seen on the Pike, and the direct testimony of the woman whom they saw with him, makes the first appearance in the neighborhood (supposing that it was he) as late as 1874. At any rate, if the real Dan Benton ever came back, it must have been after an absence of at least six years. If, in the meantime, Newby should have drifted into that country (and I have suggested some reasons which might have led him there), and started to walk, say from Franklin to Nashville, as he went pitching and tumbling along the highway like a ship in a storm, or a porpoise on the swell of a wave, nothing would be more natural than that people would say, "He walks like 'Rickety Dan.'" "There goes that 'Rickety Dan.'"

"Hello, 'Rickety Dan.'" He would come to be called "Rickety Dan" by many people, whether they believed him to be that person or not, partly because they knew no other name for him, and partly from the pure love of caricature so universal among men. Newby did not object. He doubtless thought, if he had any thoughts on the subject, that "the rose by any other name would smell as sweet," and that "Rickety Dan" was as good a name to conjure with as "Crazy Jack," or any other. In fact, he found himself more noticed and better fed under that name, and so allowed himself to be called "Rickety Dan," and called himself "Rickety Dan." The "Rickety" was dropped, and "Benton" added when away from home, or when legal or polite consideration required it.

It is a strange coincidence, of course, that Newby and Benton should have had the same rickety manner of locomotion, but this we are not expected to account for.

That Newby should have wandered into the vicinity, and received and adopted the name Dan Benton in the absence of the individual himself, is not a thing too wonderful to believe.

The heart of the whole mystery lies in this question: Did the prisoner and Lydia Benton claim the relationship of mother and son, and, if so, was it true?

We have shown how, in a very natural way, Newby might be in the neighborhood, and be called Dan Benton. If this much is capable of one reasonable solution, it is capable of others. But the question, How can the prisoner be William Newby and the son of Lydia Benton? is simply a contradiction of terms.

Taking up Newby where we left him, in the neighborhood where he had tarried on account of the name, the fame, and the attention he had received, it is reasonable to suppose that he would find his way to the hut or home of Lydia Benton. She lived near the highway, and would naturally be anxious to see the person who was nicknamed after her unfortunate boy, and who was afflicted in the same way. Her own boy had wandered away during the war, and what is more rational than to suppose that this natural object of pity should receive more than common kindness in the way of sympathy, food, and good treatment at her hands for the sake of the boy whose absence made her days lonely and her pillow hard at night? In short, as long as Newby staid around there it is not unreasonable to suppose " she treated him like a mother." Fully convinced as I am that the person is Newby, I am of the opinion that something of this kind is all the relationship that ever existed between Lydia Benton and the prisoner.

It is said that while he was in the penitentiary she called to see him, and that he sent her tobacco. It is also known that when he escaped she sent him back to prison, which she might consistently have thought best to do if he was an old, crazy, tramp acquaintance, whom she could not keep about her, and whose continued presence was likely to annoy and compromise her, but what she would not have done had he been her son. This, and his action in going straight away from home over into Indiana when released from prison, indicates that he was aware that he had "worn out his welcome" at Lydia's and proposed to cut the acquaintance. Certain it is that he never went there, nor has he been there since; and, moreover, as stated before, he never called her "mother" while in the prison.

That there has been a great mistake somewhere is admitted on all hands, and might it not have been made at this place as easily as any other?

I admit the possibility, I even think it reasonable to suppose, that Newby was in that neighborhood just after the war; that he was called Dan Benton, and that Lydia Benton treated him like a mother. Now suppose this to be the real truth of this old matter of twenty or twenty-five years' standing. Suppose a government detective should learn from penitentiary people and from Newby himself that he had served a long term at Nashville under the name of Allen Lewis, *alias* Dan Benton. Suppose he should go to Nashville and find that the man had received this name in that neighborhood from his resemblance to one Dan Benton, who was formerly known there, but who went away about the beginning of the war. Suppose he should discover that the mother of Dan Benton knew this man, and had kindly relations with him for a time— in short, as stated above, that the man had been called Dan Benton in that neighborhood, and that Lydia Benton had, in times past, treated him like a mother.

Armed with the potent authority of the government; with money more than enough for board; inspired by the prospect of the gain, notoriety, and renown which a brilliant stroke of detective work would bring him; aided by the uncertainty caused by the lapse of time, and the distracting effects of war; the task rendered easier by the contempt in which the old prison menial was held in the community, and the religious hatred of ex-Confederates towards the policy of granting pensions to Northern soldiers; the unwillingness of men to see good fortune come to those whom they have considered their inferiors; and armed with authority to offer a magnificent excursion to the North at reduced rates, with good pay attached—with all these incentives and advantages, and with the persuasive powers of the average life insurance man, *could* or *would* he have persuaded these honest people along the Granny White Pike to honestly conclude that the man who came back after the war "looked like," "was treated like," "was like," yea, WAS the *real*, original, identical Dan Benton?

The reader who has a taste for the strange and romantic, may find much food for conjecture in this wonderful case. It seems incredible that a large body of people should be absolutely mistaken as to a matter of fact and personal observation, but in this case one of two, or even three, large bodies of people is certainly mistaken. As to which is in error, the reader, from a careful perusal of the evidence, may be able to determine.

As for myself, I start out with the full conviction that the prisoner is Newby, from the appearance of the man, and from conversations that I have had with him. Though I may weigh and measure the adverse testimony and ponder over the theory of the government, yet the conviction comes back with full force, "the man is Newby, and can be no one else."

I conclude, simply, that the man was not killed at Shiloh, and that he was carried away, as he says he was, to Belle Isle. That some time after Andersonville was established, which was November 27, 1863, he was removed to that place, as stated by the seven witnesses who saw him there. When he was released, and of the history of his wanderings, we know nothing. The idea of his coming into the Sawyer settlement, advanced heretofore in this chapter, is purely hypothetical, and suggestive only of what might have taken place, and how he might have gotten the name of Daniel Benton. There seems to have been a slow but gradual dawning of the light in his mind, one idea a year perhaps, as evidenced by the successive interviews with Peter Fair.

There is a curious feature connected with the bent of this man's mind. The judge, in his in-

instructions to the jury, made the charge against Newby, in effect, that he ought to have gone to his home instead of staying in the poorhouse in Indiana. It seems that the man had some dim perception of a home and his mother. He often spoke of both, and referred to them as being in Florida. He remembered he had a mother once, for he had labored, when a boy, to support her. Both the women who testified against him stated that he spoke to them of going to his mother and his home in Florida, but, though he seemed to have some vague conception of it, he was never able to get there.

The associations with Hannah Stewart, and the birth of the two children, perhaps had a tendency to arouse some dormant recollections of his earlier domestic life. He seemed to be drifting westward, and had gotten as far as the Tennessee River, some sixty miles below Shiloh, and within a hundred miles of home, when he was sentenced for stealing the horse. Then came the long term in the penitentiary. The quiet of those years, the outside work, such as the handling of cows, and other light labor suggestive of duties about the farm, doubtless had the effect of improving his mind. At any rate, by the time he reached Indiana in 1889, he was able to give, and did give, a fuller account of himself.

His vague idea of a home in Florida began to give place to a more definite idea of his home in Illinois. In the same year his conception of the truth became strong enough to lead him vaguely, and finally brought him to Illinois, and under the observation of some of the men who knew him in days long gone by.

From this point the story has already been told.

Having been induced by his old friends and comrades to apply for a pension, an agent of the government was set to work on the case. The special agent McBride, when put upon the case, as before stated, followed back the story as Newby was able to relate it, through poorhouse and prison, got in among the Sawyers and their relatives, who were employes at the prison, and some of whom served time. From these he learned the story of "Rickety Dan" Benton, and set to work to connect the two. He came to White County, and, under the pretense of further identification, gets the consent of the old wife and sons of Newby to let him go to Tennessee. Newby was willing to go anywhere for the purpose of having his identity established, "for," said he, "if I ain't Newby, who in the hell am I?"

The writer was on the train when he was being taken away. He went voluntarily, for I talked with him and the agent both, and McBride said that it was a great point in favor of the genuineness of Newby's claim that he was willing to go anywhere and to confront anybody.

The old man was taken down there, and, of course, he was known to those who served in the penitentiary under any capacity. He told Lem Sawyer that if he took him back to jail that he would kill him if he went to hell for it. McBride put him on exhibition—put him through his gaits. "Yes," everybody said, "it's the fellow that was in the penitentiary—he has the same rickety walk." Old man Wooten, who had not seen "Rickety Dan" since he put him in the poorhouse, did not recognize him until the agent walked the old cripple up and down, and then he was prepared to come to Springfield and swear it was "Rickety Dan."

When a sufficient number of people were secured who would swear that it was not Newby, he was brought back to Illinois, and, instead of being restored to his home, as the promise was, he was taken to Springfield and thrown into jail as an impostor. It is said that the agent claims as an excuse for his acting in bad faith with the old man, that he promised not to bring him back home, but to "bring him back to Illinois," a subterfuge which when played upon a crazy man and a crazy man's family is beneath the contempt of any fair-minded person.

It will be well to remark that by working secretly, as is the manner of United States detectives, this "Dan Benton" theory was sprung upon the friends of Newby at a time when they had neither the time nor the means to investigate, but that efforts are being made to the end that the truth, wherever it lies, may be determined.

THE LAWYERS.

WILLIAM E. SHUTT.

William E. Shutt, present United States Attorney for this district, assisted by the Hon. John G. Drennen, represented the government in the prosecution of this case. Mr. Shutt was born in in Loudon County, Va., is about fifty years old, and has been practicing law at Springfield since 1863. First was member of the firm of Robinson, Napp & Shutt; since in the firm composed of United States Senator Palmer and son, with himself. At present the firm is Palmer, Shutt & Drennen. Mr. Shutt has enjoyed some of the honors of politics. He was twelve years state senator, and one term mayor of his own city of Springfield. He possesses many types of a model son of the Old Dominion. A giant in physical appearance, of fine form and presence. In his management of a case he both drives and coaxes. He has a fine sense of duty, and in this case exerted all the powers he possessed to convict his man.

JOHN G. DRENNEN.

John G. Drennen was born December 3, 1856, in Caldwell County, Ky., and came to Illinois when a boy. He has been practicing law since 1880. Was State's Attorney of Christian County from 1880 to 1888, and was master in chancery for the same county. Mr. Drennen, as you see, has been eating plums most of the years since his admission to the bar. At present he resides in Springfield. John is a typical Kentuckian, except he has no broad-brimmed-hat foolishness about him. He is generous, kind and good-looking. He is sharp as lightning, makes points or sees them quickly, and has the faculty of making the jury see them as he does. He is very swift. You would like him. Old Newby was almost sharp enough to fear Drennen when he got before that jury.

The claimant was ably defended by J. R. Creighton, E. C. Kramer, George W. Johns, and E. S. Robinson.

J. R. CREIGHTON.

Mr. Creighton was born in White County, Ill., forty-four years ago, and has been practicing law eighteen years in Fairfield, Wayne County, and adjoining counties. He was candidate for attorney general on the ticket with Gen. Palmer, and is well known in Illinois. He is a brother of Judge James A. Creighton, of Springfield. Mr. Creighton is an almost invincible defender of a man charged with crime, contests closely, pushes the fight, covers his retreat, and sometimes sallies forth with great power.

COL. GEO. W. JOHNS

Was born in Albion, Edwards County, Ill., is forty-five years old, and was admitted to the bar in 1870. He located first at Carmi, but came to Fairfield in 1873, where he has since remained. Mr. Johns is a good lawyer and a safe counselor, worthy the confidence which people repose in him. He is public-spirited, and a benefit to the community in which he lives.

E. C. KRAMER.

E. C. Kramer was born in Wabash County, Ill., and came to Wayne County when a boy. He is thirty years old, and has been practicing law eight years. He has been county judge one term. At present he is one of the commissioners of the Southern Illinois Penitentiary. He is well and favorably known. He is a bright, solid man, a good lawyer, and enjoys a good practice.

E. S. ROBINSON

Was born in Fairfield, Ill., and is twenty-five years old. Has been practicing law three years at Springfield, Ill. He is a son of the Hon. Wm. H. Robinson, deceased, who for many years was on the board of railroad and warehouse commissioners. Ned had charge of the preparation of the case at the capital. He is an industrious, honest, competent young lawyer of much promise.

It may be said of this case that no case was ever tried in any court that excited more comment by the psess of the country, and more intense interest by the people in general, than the Newby case. No, not in all history. Inch by inch it was contested. Unequal—only an old, demented, crippled, impoverished man to cope with a great government like the United States in the contest. Yet was the principle involved, "Is he Newby or is he Benton?"

One of the most competent special examiners, Mr. McBride, was put upon this case by the government, with all the time and money necessary at his command. Well did he push the prosecution. A scapegoat must be had, and Dan Benton, the " great Unaccountable," was furnished as an imaginary, whose trifling life from his birth must be apologized for by poor old Newby, in his demented condition, for which he is no more responsible than was the unfortunate scapegoat for the anathemas thrust upon him for his misfortunes — born rickety, and with a wobbling gait the only analogy.

JAMES MC'CARTNEY.

Mr. McCartney was born in Trumbull County, Ohio, in the year 1835. He studied law with Judge Burchard, of Warren, and when admitted, moved to Galva, Henry County, Ill. Here he entered the army early in 1861 in one of the first Illinois regiments, and remained with it until the close of hostilities. On his return from the army he removed from Galva and came to Fairfield, in Wayne County, in 1866. Here he continued to practice his profession with much success until elected attorney general of the state ten years ago. This position he filled with honor to himself and to the satisfaction of the people of the state. The General now lives in Chicago, and follows his profession, his office being in the Unity Building.

Upon hearing the astonishing verdict in the Newby case, Gen. McCartney at once tendered his services to assist his poor, unfortunate neighbor to get a new trial, or to press the case to the highest court in the land for review. Mr. McCartney is in the case to stay, and this without fee or reward, except the reward that comes from such an act prompted by so pure a motive.

WM. E. SHUTT. JOHN G. DRENNEN.
ATTORNEYS WHO PROSECUTED CLAIMANT.

CHAPTER VIII.

THE TRIAL.

ON Saturday, April 29, 1893, the claimant, William Newby, was taken to Springfield by Thomas H. McBride, special pension examiner, and there placed under arrest and lodged in jail, upon a charge of "presenting a fraudulent pension claim." His family and friends in White, Wayne, and Edwards Counties were notified of his arrest, and at once commenced preparing for his defense. Newby remained in jail until May 20, when he was released on two thousand dollars bond.

At the June term of the United States District Court the claimant was indicted by the grand jury under the name of Daniel Benton, *alias* William Newby, on three charges, viz., presenting a fraudulent pension claim, perjury, and making false affidavit in pension claim, and his trial was set for July 11.

In the meantime his relatives and friends in the southern part of the state were busy hunting evidence and raising money to pay the expenses of his defense. Owing to the poverty of the defendant, and the general hard times, but a few hundred dollars was raised, and the defense was badly handicapped in preparing for the trial on account of insufficient funds. The trial was to be held in Springfield, nearly one hundred and fifty miles from the home of Newby and his neighbors. There was railroad fare, and board while in Springfield, to pay in cash, and also the time that the witnesses were away from their various occupations, to take into consideration. The government would furnish the defendant but ten witnesses, and they must live in Illinois. He needed about two hundred, some of the most important of whom lived in Arkansas, Missouri, Indiana, and other states. To obtain all these witnesses would necessitate an expenditure of perhaps three thousand dollars.

The defendant's family and friends were able to raise only about one fifth of that amount, and, as a natural consequence, he had to go to trial without many of his most important witnesses.

Although it was very hot and dusty and most unpleasant to travel on the day before the 11th, one hundred and fifty of Newby's old friends and neighbors went to Springfield at their own expense to testify in his behalf.

Notwithstanding the intense heat, the large United States court-room was crowded to overflowing long before court time, by an expectant audience, anxious to hear every word of this wonderful case.

The Springfield daily papers had been filled for weeks with articles about the case, all assuming the defendant to be an impostor, and a strong prejudice had been worked up against him.

It is safe to say that everybody in Springfield who had read the papers believed him to be a fraud. This opinion underwent a great change before the trial was concluded, and public sentiment was almost unanimously changed in favor of the defendant.

The government was represented by United States District Attorney W. E. Shutt and Hon. John G. Drennen, law partner of Senator John M. Palmer.

The defendant's attorneys were Hon. Jacob R. Creighton, Judge E. C. Kramer, and Col. George W. Johns, of Fairfield, Ill., and E. S. Robinson, of Springfield. Judge J. W. Allen presided on the bench.

When court was opened, both the prosecution and defense announced their readiness for trial, and, after the usual preliminary motions, etc., the work of selecting a jury was begun, which occupied all the morning and part of the afternoon.

After the jury was selected, Mr. Shutt made the opening statement for the prosecution in an hour's address.

Mr. Shutt said that the defendant was an impostor from beginning to end. That he was not William Newby, and never heard of William Newby until the spring of 1891, when he happened to be in Hamilton County, Ill., and heard of the death of William Newby at Shiloh, and then concluded to perpetrate this fraud, intimating that there was someone behind the defendant assisting him in the plot. On the contrary, he was a Tennessee adventurer, named Daniel Benton, who was born in his present crippled condition, and, from his walk, was always known as "Rickety Dan." He would trace him, step by step, from the time he was a very small child, only four or five years of age, in Williamson County in 1849, until the present time, never skipping more than a year or two of his life at a time. He said the government would trace him from the time he left Williamson County in 1862 or '64, year by year, until 1877, when he was sent to the Tennessee state penitentiary from Benton County for horse-stealing, where he remained as a prisoner until 1889, when he was discharged, having served out his time, and would show, beyond any question of doubt, by a large array of witnesses that this defendant was no other, and could be no other, than Daniel Benton. He would also account for the so-called severe injury on the side of his head by proving that he received that by being struck by the rebound of a wagon-bow in Tennessee in about 1861 or '62. Moreover, he would prove, to the satisfaction of everyone, that William Newby was killed at the battle of Shiloh, and his body afterwards buried, and, no difference who this defendant is, he can not be Bill Newby.

Mr. Shutt, during his address, became greatly excited, and, turning to the large array of defendant's witnesses, said that he would convince every one of them, before the government's evidence was concluded, that the defendant was a colossal fraud, playing upon the credulities of the people, and that they had been basely imposed upon.

Mr. Creighton followed Mr. Shutt for the defense. He said the defense would introduce scores of William Newby's relatives and old neighbors, who were intimate with him before the war, and many of his army comrades, who positively identify the defendant as the original William Newby. That ninety-nine out of every hundred of his old friends who had made any effort to test this man knew beyond any question of doubt that he was none other than their old friend and comrade. His old mother, now ninety-one years of age, who brought him into this world, had come here through the dust and heat to testify for her son. His wife, who had shared his every thought in their lonely log home for many long years, and had borne him six children, and mortgaged her home, and, together with their children, had come to help this poor old physical and mental wreck, whom they knew to be husband and father. It was not a question of pension with them, for the pension department, in its wisdom, had long since refused to grant the defendant any pension. It was a question of whether or not their husband and father, who had left home and family to answer to his country's call, and had a thousand times more than given his life in its service, should now be locked up in a felon's cell for attempting, in his old age, to obtain a small recompense for his services.

It would also be shown by the defense that this defendant was, for many months, confined in that southern hell, Andersonville prison, as a prisoner of war. He was totally insane while there, rotten with the scurvy, and covered with vermin. It is no wonder that his mind was a wreck, and that he did not return home sooner. Many old soldiers, who had never heard of Bill Newby, will tell you that they knew this defendant in Andersonville, and that he was there known as "Crazy Jack," a poor object of pity, even among all that miserable crowd of prisoners.

It will be shown to you that in the same regiment that Bill Newby belonged to there was a soldier named Hiram Morris, who was, in size and appearance, very much like William Newby; in fact, his muster-roll fits that of Newby. Hiram Morris was in that famous charge at the battle of Shiloh on Sunday morning. He was reported missing after that charge, and he has never been heard of since. His widow still lives near William Newby's old home, and could never obtain a pension because she could not prove his death. The bodies of those killed that Sunday morning were left in the hot southern sun until Tuesday evening, when they were hurriedly buried by their comrades. Their bodies were swollen and black. It would be hard to tell one person from another in that condition, and, in the hurry of the burial, made a mistake and buried the body of Hiram Morris for William Newby. Newby's comrades, at that battle, saw him receive a gun-shot wound in the right thigh. Also a wound in the left side of the head, caused by a piece of a shell. This defendant has the scars left by those wounds.

Moreover, the defense will introduce every physician who has examined the defendant, including five physicians whom the government had examine him, and they will tell you that this defendant never had the rickets, that he was a mature man before he became a cripple. Also, that the scar in his head was left by a wound that has injured his skull, and affects his mind and memory. He can not be Daniel Benton, then, who was crippled from birth, and suffered from the disease known as "rickets" all his life.

William Newby had a long scar on his right foot, caused by a broadaxe; another on his shin, where he was kicked by a colt, and another on the left arm, left there from a severe bite which he received in a fight. He also had two moles on his face, one near the right eye, the other on the right side of his upper lip.

This defendant has all those scars and those two moles.

As the reader will discover, there were three lines on which the government introduced testimony. First, that the defendant is Daniel Benton; second, that William Newby was killed at Shiloh, and, whoever this defendant is, he can not be William Newby. Third, relatives and neighbors who knew William Newby have seen this man, and, whether Newby was killed at Shiloh or not, claimant is not Newby.

The defense had four branches. First, the defendant is William Newby; second, it was Hiram Morris, killed at Shiloh, and not William Newby; third, the defendant was a prisoner of war in Andersonville prison, known as "Crazy Jack," and was then about thirty-eight or forty years old, and therefore can not be the original Dan Benton, who was but a boy during the war; fourth, the defendant never had the rickets, and was a mature man before he became a cripple, and therefore can not be Dan Benton, who was crippled from birth, and was always afflicted with the rickets.

At the conclusion of Mr. Creighton's address

the government introduced two witnesses, A. M. Wilson and J. H. Upchurch, of McLeansboro, Ill., to prove the making of the affidavit by the defendant. Both thought he was of sound mind at the time of making the application.

John Sawyer, of Tennessee, aged eighty-five, was the first important witness introduced. He said that he first became acquainted with the defendant, who was known as Dan Banton, not Benton, in Williamson County, Tenn., where he lived in 1859, when Dan was a small boy. He was then afflicted with the rickets, and crippled the same way he is now. He was known as "Rickety Dan," from his physical condition. Knew him up till a year or so after the war commenced, when he left that country. He was then a young boy. Next saw him in the Tenneessee state penitentiary in about 1880, where I was a guard and defendant was a prisoner. Positive this is the boy raised in Williamson County.

Mrs. Bettie Fudge, daughter of John Sawyer, gave her age as forty-eight. Went to school with Dan Benton, or Banton, when both were little children. Knew him until during the war, when he was twelve to fifteen years old. Did not see Dan after early part of war until the summer of 1868, when he passed her house on Granny White's Pike, with two women. He then looked to be thirty years old. Next saw him, about 1884, in penitentiary at Nashville. Defendant is, undoubtedly, Dan Banton.

W. K. McDowell, Williamson County, Tenn., aged forty-four, knew Dan Benton four or five years before the war. Witness was five or six years old when he first became acquainted with him, and Dan was about ten. Knew him until the war, when Dan left there. Next saw him in 1868, with two women, on Granny White's Pike. Did not speak to him then — merely passed him on the road. Dan looked about thirty years old then. Next saw him this spring, when McBride took him to Tennessee. Did not recognize him until McBride said it was Dan Benton. No doubt as to identity.

Willis Sawyer, Mrs. Angelina Sawyer, Richard M. McDaniel, Thos. S. Waller, Wm. J. Gresham, James W. Talkington, J. B. McCrory, Riley Alley, Robert D. Waller, all testified to having known Dan Benton, or Banton, when he was a small child, up till 1862 or '63, when he was twelve to fifteen years old. He was always crippled. Had rickets, and was known as "Rickety Dan." They all saw him in 1868, walking along Granny White's Pike with two women. Did not speak to him. He appeared to be about thirty years old.

Moreover, it was later shown by the prosecution that the defendant did not know the two women in question until late in the fall of 1872; that they were in Indiana until the fall of 1873, and could not have been in Tennessee until the summer of 1874, or later. The writer is unable to understand why these positive witnesses all agreed upon the summer of 1868 as being the time when they saw Dan Benton on Granny White's Pike, and yet all are at least six years mistaken.

Washington Bonds, of Nashville, Tenn., aged forty-seven, knew Dan Benton when both were small boys. "Saw him in 1861 at my father's house. He wasn't doing anything, just happened to come. Saw him in 1865 about a mile from Hillsboro, riding a mare. He had on a dark suit. Saw him in 1867 or '68 on Granny White's Pike, between seven and eight miles from Nashville. He was going north. I asked him where he was going. He said he was going back to Illinois. I called him Dan. He called me Wash. I next saw him in prison at Nashville, about twelve or fourteen years ago."

Question by Attorney: "How long have you lived in Nashville?"

Answer: "I think about fourteen years."

"Did you ever move away from Tennessee?"

"Yes, I moved to Texas, I think in 1870, but do not know."

Willis Sawyer, Jos. Talkington, Edward Wells, J. W. Alley, Thos. S. Waller, James W. Talkington, Wm. J. Sawyer, Lem Sawyer and Richard McDaniel all saw defendant in the penetentiary at Nashville between 1880 and 1889, and positively identify him as the original Dan Benton, whom they knew as a small boy.

Walter P. Alley, Nashville, Tennessee, aged forty-six, "knew Dan Benton when both were small boys. Dan was helping bend a wagon-bow at my father's blacksmith-shop about 1861. Some one let loose of the bow, and it rebounded, striking Dan on the left side of the head, making a deep wound. Dan was then about thirteen years old. Wound healed rapidly, and caused him no trouble. The bow was sixteen feet long, six inches wide, and one half inch thick. Dan was always 'rickety.' Walks better now than he did then. Have never seen him since, until the present time. Didn't know his last name. Positive defendant is the same person."

J. W. Alley, Frank C. Holly, and James H. Alley also testified to seeing Dan Benton receive a wound by wagon-bow striking him.

Robert H. Hill, Williamson County, Tenn., "saw Dan Benton at Lem Sawyer's once during the war, some time during the war, I think, about 1864. Had a short conversation with him. He was then about fifteen years old. Never spoke to him but that once. Have never seen him since, until present time."

Question; "Have you any doubts that this defendant is Dan Benton?"

Answer: "None in the world, sir."

Robert A. Read, Walter P. Alley, Frank C. Holly, Thomas Buntham, James H. Alley, George Mayfield, Wm. Callender, and G. W. Morgan, all knew Dan Benton from a few years before the war until about 1862. Have never seen him since, until the present time. Have no doubt the defendant is Dan Benton.

Andrew Wooton, Williamson County, Tenn. "Born and raised there. Lived a few years in White County, Ill., Dan Banton with me and my mother. Moved back to Tennessee, but don't know when. Dan and his mother went to Tennessee with me. I knew him four or five years before the war, in Tennessee. I took Dan to the Williamson County poorfarm before the war. Never saw him afterwards until the spring of 1893, when McBride brought him to my house. McBride asked me if I knew this man. I said I thought maybe I did, but asked McBride to let him walk. After he walked I said, 'It is Dan Benton.' Dan did not recognize me."

This ended the Tennessee witnesses, and Peter R. Farr, a crippled but very intelligent inmate of the Pike County, Ind., poorfarm, was next placed on the stand. He testified in substance as follows:

"I have been in the Pike County poorfarm twenty-five years. First saw the defendant in in latter part of 1868, when he came to the poorfarm. Defendant then gave his name as Allen Lewis. He staid some time and left, but came back in 1870, and said his name was Dan Benton. He again returned in 1872 as Dan Benton, and again in the spring of 1874, under the name of Dan Benton. He staid about five weeks the last time, and went away with Hannah Stewart, an inmate of the poorfarm. He then staid away until the spring of 1889, when he returned, and said he had been in the Tennessee penitentiary. He told me in the spring of 1889 that he was known as Dan Benton, Allen Allen, Allen Lewis, and John Baker, that he used to be called "Crazy Jack," and over in Illinois used to be known as Bill Newby."

This witness was a surprise and a disappointment to the prosecution, as it maintained that the defendant never heard of Newby until the spring of 1891. He was recalled by the defense, and proved a very valuable witness, as will be shown later.

Hannah Stewart "first met defendant about twenty-one years ago in the Pike County, Ind., poorfarm. He was then known as Dan Benton. Left the poorfarm with Dan in 1873. Then had one son by my husband, Stewart. That son is a cripple. I am crippled. I traveled with defendant about five years. Had two children by him. One is dead. The other is present. He is a boy. Is crippled and subject to fits. It was over a year after we left the poorfarm until we got to Tennessee. While in Tennessee, had another woman with us."

Several other witnesses from various points in Indiana and Ohio tried to prove that defendant was in poorhouses throughout those two states under the name of Dan Benton.

This concluded the first and most important branch of the prosecution. Two witnesses testified that they had seen Newby dead after the battle of Shiloh, and helped bury his remains. Their evidence is important, and, no doubt, will be interesting to the reader.

W. H. Merritt, farmer, Wayne County, Ill.: "Knew William Newby for about five years before the war, living six miles from him. Belonged to the same company in the army. Newby joined the company at Camp Butler, near Springfield, Ill. Saw him at Camp Butler, Jefferson Barracks, Cairo, Bird's Point, and Shiloh. Newby was a big man, with round face, fat hands. Defendant has no resemblance to Newby except in the eyes. Dr. R. H. Maricle and I were not in the battle of Shiloh after the beginning of the first charge, but were in the rear, and were captured by the Confederates. Were afterwards recaptured by the Federal army. G. J. George, orderly sergeant, Company D, told me that Newby was dead. I was detailed to help bury the dead late Monday evening. Found Newby's body, and buried it. He was shot in the forehead, just over one eye."

Dr. R. H. Maricle, White County, Ill., physician and farmer. "Acquainted with Newby from childhood. In the same company in the army. Saw him every day in the company.

Was detailed at Shiloh to help bury the dead of Company D. Was informed that Newby was killed Sunday morning, and when we went to bury the bodies, saw Newby's body. Helped lay his body in the trench, then cut the names of those who were buried on a board, and put it at the head of the trench. Nothing about the defendant that resembles Newby. Don't think defendant is him. Newby was of heavy build, large bones, good-sized face, biggest fist I ever saw, hair dark brown, beard lighter than hair, hazel eyes, fair complexion, short neck, short fingers.

Cross examination: "Buried the bodies on Tuesday evening."

The following letter was then submitted to the witness:

MILL SHOALS, ILL., April 21, 1891.
Mrs. Ferby Newby, Claud, Texas.

On or about April 9, 1862, I wrote to you from Shiloh, Tenn., that your husband, William Newby, was killed on April 6, 1862 (now a little over twenty-nine years ago), stating what I felt were positive facts in the case, and which I would certify to in any court every day since that time until now. I told you just how I had him laid down by Uncle Adam Files, and had his name cut on a pine board, with a spear pointing to position he occupied in the soldier grave. I also cut the names of Adam Files, Holloway Beard, Eustrich Willit, John Raner, and Hamilton Farmer. As you are aware that a man has been identified and is now at home with his family and brothers as the identical William Newby, of Company D, 40th Illinois Infantry Volunteers, and not until I visited him the third time could I be reconciled that he was the man that I supposed I had helped to bury over twenty-nine years ago, although the evidence of his identity was preponderous. Come home and see him, and be convinced what your friends have been wiring and writing to you about is straight goods. You need not expect him to look just as he did on August 8, 1861, when him and I, with the rest of our brothers, neighbors and friends, bid farewell to those who were near and dear to us, and went out to defend the stars and stripes, which our forefathers had declared should wave over the land of the free and the home of the brave, which had been torn down by traitors, and our Union people murdered outright. Everything points to proofs which are undeniable, but there is a great change in his looks, of course, but, according to his statement, hs has been in those prison dens which human tongue can not describe, and, after the close of the war, was held or prohibited from coming home to keep him from getting a pension, and was compelled, under the lash, to vote the rebel ticket. No wonder, then, there is such a change in his looks. His scars all conform to the identity of him, both those he had when he enlisted, and those he got in the army. He has only lost one tooth, and that is the back jaw-tooth on the upper jaw and the right side. I want to tell you, Ferby, it was hard for me to be convinced, but now I am satisfied, and hope you will not think hard of me for writing the letter of his death, identity, and burial, April 9, 1862, and I don't want to put any more wooden tombstones to soldiers' graves after making such a blunder as I and the rest of the comrades did; and now I congratulate you on the privilege of seeing your husband, who was so devoted to you. I am, as ever,

Your friend,
R. H. MARICLE.

Question: "Did you write the letter?"
Answer: "Yes, sir."

"How many times had you seen and talked with defendant before you wrote the letter?"

"I wrote it after about the fourth time I had visited him."

"Did you then believe it was Newby?"

"Yes, sir, I think I did, but wrote the letter because I thought my pension and property was threatened."

At the conclusion of Dr. Maricle's testimony, the prosecution took up the third branch of its case and introduced two brothers, one sister of Newby's, and twelve of his neighbors, who do not know of their own knowledge that he was killed, but do not recognize the defendant as Newby.

None of these witnesses, except the brothers and sister, had paid much attention to the defendant, and merely said that they did not recognize him. They all agreed that defendant does not answer to the description of William Newby when he went into the army. They all described Newby as about five feet, eleven inches high, large frame, weight about one hundred and seventy pounds, rather slender hands, medium-sized face, ordinary neck, small, brown eyes, and almost black hair mixed with white.

Carroll Newby, brother of William Newby, an

inmate of the Jefferson County poorhouse: "I am about seventy-one years old. My brother William would be about sixty-eight years if alive. The defendant came to Jefferson County poorfarm in February, 1890. He called himself Allen Benton. Said he lived in Florida, and had been in the Confederate army. Do not recognize him as brother Bill. He does not look like brother Bill used to."

Mrs. Perlina Campbell, sister of William Newby: "I am affected with a disease in the head, and my memory has been spoiled. This man does not look like brother Bill. When the defendant first came to White County in the spring of 1891 I went to see him several times, and talked to him and believed it was my brother, but do not now."

Question; "Do you remember of Bill cutting his foot badly with a broadaxe?"

Answer: "Yes, have heard the family talk about it."

"Do you remember of him being kicked on the shin by a colt, which left a large scar?"

"Yes, sir, I think so."

"Do you remember of him being bit on the arm in a fight?"

"I remember hearing the family talk about it."

Presley Newby, brother of William Newby: "Don't know age, but think about sixty-four. Don't think defendant is my brother. He does not look like Bill did. Bill had dark-auburn hair, and wore it long, and in summer the ends would sunburn, and make his hair look lighter. This man's hair is darker than Bill's was. My hair used to be red, but has turned dark. My hair used to be redder than Bill's (Presley now has dark-brown hair). Bill had small, brown eyes."

Cross examination—Question: "When it was first reported in your neighborhood that Bill had returned did you not describe to Ki Newby how Bill ought to look, and tell him if it was Bill he would have a long scar on one foot, where he had been cut by a broadaxe, another on the shin caused by a colt kicking him, another on the arm, where he was bitten in a fight, and a mole on the right side of the upper lip?"

"I think I did. When I first saw defendant, did not believe it was Bill, but after talking to him thought he was, but now don't believe he is. When I first saw the defendant, I thought I would test him, and asked him if he had ever rafted any. He said, 'Yes, brother Jim and I rafted on White River before the war. There was an Irishman with us who died, and I started to shave him. While shaving him, the dead man threw up his arm, and I dropped the razor and run. Afterwards, while running our raft down the river, it broke in two, and we lost part of it.' All that had happened to brother Bill, but I thought I would question him further, and asked him if he had ever had any fights. He said, 'Yes, I had a fight with a man in Liberty once, and he bit me on the arm.' He then told about a fight he had in a meadow near there, naming the meadow. Bill had both of those fights."

"Did you not tell John Powell, W. A. Jordan, and others, that the defendant was undoubtedly your brother?"

"Yes, sir."

"Did you not tell Thomas Allen and Joseph Creighton that it would pay Bill to give you about five hundred dollars?"

"Yes, I believe I did."

J. R. CREIGHTON.   E. C. KRAMER.

ATTORNEYS FO

GEO. W. JOHNS.   E. S. ROBINSON.

THE DEFENSE.

CHAPTER IX.

THE DEFENSE.

DAY by day, as the government presented its evidence, the interest in the trial grew in intensity, and by Friday evening, when the government closed, it was at an extremely high pitch.

On Saturday morning it was announced in all the Springfield papers that the defense had begun, and long before time for court to convene that morning people were flocking to the Federal building, and when Commissioner Kidd opened court at 8:30 o'clock every available foot of room was occupied. This intense interest continued throughout the trial, and after about the third day of the defense there was a complete revolution of public sentiment in favor of the claimant.

Each day, from early morning until late at night, groups of people stood around discussing the events of the prosecution and defense.

Often the bebater became greatly excited, and often trouble was narrowly averted between the witnesses from Tennessee, many of whom had served under Gen. Forrest in the Confederate army, and the partisans of the claimant, a majority of whom had given years of their life to the Union.

All the prejudices and bitterness of the late war were revived, and it seems remarkable to the author that the two weeks of the trial passed without trouble.

This feeling ran so high, and the excitement became so great, that on Wednesday, the fourth day of the defense, the court placed two officers in charge of the jury, which heretofore had been allowed perfect freedom when not in the courtroom, with orders not to allow the members to talk to anyone.

Wherever the author would go, up and down the street, in the hotels, stores, and work-shops, he would hear the name of Newby. The claimant and his case seemed to be the sole topic of conversation in the capital city, and a familiar greeting on the street was, "Is he Newby or Benton?"

There were one hundred and forty witnesses introduced for the defense. It would, of course, be tedious to the reader to read the evidence of each witness, as most of them testified only upon one point, identifying the defendant as William Newby, whom they knew before and in the war. Newby's wife, his mother, a brother, two sisters, and seventeen other relatives positively identified the claimant as William Newby. Seventy-six old neighbors and thirty-seven members of the 40th Regiment swore that he was William Newby beyond question of doubt. His relations, and many of the other witnesses, had known him for a great many years. A large number of these people had been connected with William Newby before the war, or in the army, in matters that were only known to the witness and William Newby. Each one had not only recognized the claimant as William Newby by his appearance and manner, but had applied severe tests to him. He was able to meet these tests to the satisfaction of every witness.

C. C. Maulding, of Wayne County, was the first witness for the defense. "I was a member of Company D, 40th Illinois Infantry, the company that William Newby belonged to. Knew Newby well in the army from about the 12th of August, 1861, until the first day of the battle of Shiloh, April 6, 1862. Stood on guard with him several times. Was intimate with him. Was with him often. The first time I saw him after the battle of Shiloh was in February or March, 1991, in a hardware store at Wayne City. I could not identify him by merely seeing him, but did after talking to him. He told me incidents that had occurred between him and me. I think his mind is in a bad condition. I have no doubt that defendant is William Newby."

John Haefle, merchant, Burnt Prairie, Ill.: "I was well acquainted with William Newby, from the spring of 1853 until he joined the army in 1861. I lived about four miles from Newby. He was then a large man, with dark complexion, dark eyes, and dark hair, nearly black. Neck in proportion to balance of his body. Pretty well developed through shoulders. He had an impediment in his speech, a sort of stutter, and a general Newby voice. He has the same peculiar voice and stutter now. I first saw Newby after he went to the war about a week after his return in 1891. Have seen him and talked with him several times."

Question: "Is the defendant William Newby?"

"Yes, sir, that is Bill Newby; not a bit of doubt."

"Do you recognize him from his appearance or from conversations had with him?"

"Both."

Ezekiah Huntsinger: "Knew William Newby well up to the time he entered the army. Have seen him several times since his return in 1891. Haven't a doubt but that this is Newby. Am able to identify him from general appearance and conversations. The more I see him, the more natural he becomes as Newby, and the more I know he is Newby. He resembles the Newby family very forcibly in manner. I think his mind is in a very bad condition."

John Felix, White County: "I have been intimately acquainted with Newby since he was a boy. Lived about five miles from him until he joined the army. He was then about five feet eleven inches tall, and weighed about one hundred and seventy or one hundred and eighty pounds. Had black hair, dark complexion, and dark eyes. Neck in proportion to body. Had a tolerably broad hand, fingers not short and stumpy. Saw Newby the Sunday after Ki brought him home on Tuesday. Have seen and talked with him many times since. His mind is bad, but sometimes comes and goes."

Question: "Is this defendant William Newby?"

"He is the William Newby I knew, and nobody else."

"Have you any doubt?"

"No doubt at all."

"Do you recognize him from his appearance, or from conversations had with him?"

"From appearance."

David E. Felix: "I was intimately acquainted with William Newby from the time he was big enough to run around until he enlisted in the army. He was then a large, full-fleshed man, dark-complected, dark hair, dark eyes. Have seen him several times since he returned in 1891, and recognize him. Can see a strong resemblance to his mother and the Simpsons (Newby's mother was a Simpson). He also looks like his father, John Newby, used to. Have heard him talk to other people, but have had no conversation with him. He has the same talk, manner, and general appearance that he had before the war. I have no doubt that he is William Newby."

"Do you recognize him from his appearance?"

"Yes, sir."

Mrs. Julia A. Rogers: "I knew Newby well before the war. Lived about two miles from him. He then had dark eyes and dark complexion. His hair was black on top of his head when it was protected by his hat, but he wore it long, and it looked sunburned on the end. He had a fleshy neck. I saw defendant soon after his return two years ago, and have seen him since. I recognized him by my recollection of him before the war. Recognize him by his looks. It is Bill Newby. There is no doubt at all."

Wm. Greathouse, brother-in-law to William Newby: "I was raised with Bill Newby, and married his sister. Before the war he had dark-brown hair, dark-brown eyes, and dark complexion, large hands and short fingers. He was a big-boned man. I remember him cutting his foot with a broadaxe, being kicked by a colt, and being bit on the arm in a fight before the war. Have examined him since his return, and find all the scars on him. From the defendant's actions, appearance, and conversation I am positive that he is William Newby."

Thompson Wallace, aged sixty-eight: "William Newby and I were raised together, and were in the army together. He had dark eyes, dark hair, and dark complexion. Was about five feet eleven inches tall, and was rather fleshy."

"Is the defendant William Newby?"

"That is William Newby, certain as my name is Thompson Wallace."

James McNeely: "I belonged to the same company that William Newby did in the army, and I was well acquainted with him. I saw him on Sunday morning at the battle of Shiloh. I heard after the first charge Sunday morning that Newby had been killed, also several others of Company D, and went in the field and looked for Newby's body. I found the bodies of seven or eight of Company D among the dead, but could not find Newby. No bodies were buried until Tuesday evening. The defendant is William Newby beyond a doubt."

Robert Scott: "I was in the same company with Newby in the army and was with him every day. I first saw him, after his return, in Fairfield. He knew me and called me by name, and I recognized him. This man is Bill Newby."

Captain James T. Vaught, Enfield, Ill.: "I knew William Newby from my earliest recollection until he went to the war, and also saw him in the army. He had dark hair, dark eyes with yellowish cast, and dark, swarthy complexion. Saw him in April, 1891, for the first time after his return. Have seen and talked to defendant twenty-five times since that, and can have no doubt that he is William Newby."

Cross-examination: "Do you recognize him from his appearance or from conversations had with him?"

"Principally from conversations, but some from appearance."

Peter Fair recalled by defense. "In 1868, while defendant was in the Pike County, Ind., poorhouse, under the name of Allen Lewis, I heard him say he was shot in the thigh at Shiloh. At another time in 1872, in the same poorhouse, he said that he was a Union soldier, and was at the battle of Shiloh, where he was shot in the leg and was also hurt in the head by a piece of a bomb-shell. He said that the hurt in the head had made him crazy. After that he talked about being at Shiloh, and said that the hurt in his head had made him crazy, and that he used to be known as 'Crazy Jack.' At another place he used to be known as Allen Allen, and over in Illinois he used to be known as Bill Newby."

John Tombs: "I knew Newby all my life, until he went to the war, living about three miles from him. I recollect his appearance very well. He was nearly six feet tall, and of strong build, weighing about one hundred and ninety pounds. He had dark hair, dark eyes, and dark complexion. Saw the defendant the next morning after his return. Have seen and talked with him several times since, and we have talked over our early life. He looks like he did before the war. There is no doubt about him being Newby."

Mrs. John Tombs, aged fifty-three: "I knew William Newby from the time I was fifteen years old until the war. Lived for a while at his house. He had dark hair, dark eyes, and dark complexion. I saw him about the third day after his return in 1891. Have talked with him a half dozen times since. I knew him from his looks.

Cross-examination: "Newby had a large hand and foot, big neck, and a fat face."

Wm. Howard: "I lived close to Newby, and knew him well before the war. Can remember his appearance. The defendant is William Newby. He has William Newby's face. The more I look at him the more I know it is Newby."

Cross-examination: "Newby had a medium-sized hand for a man of his size. He had a large neck, that is, it was fleshy. He would weigh a hundred and eighty pounds or more. I don't know that I could have identified the defendant at first sight, but after looking at him carefully, and hearing his voice, know he is William Newby."

J. R. Buchannan: "I knew William Newby for about thirty years before the war. He was a big, stout man, weighing about two hundred pounds, had a big, fleshy neck, dark hair, dark eyes, and dark complexion. I saw him soon after his return in 1891. Have seen him frequently since then. He has the same voice, same eyes, and same expression of the face. I have talked over incidents that happened to him and me before the war with him. I am able to recognize him. I remember the time he was cut in the foot by a broadaxe, and also remember him being kicked on the shin by a colt."

Mrs. Polly Storey: "I knew Newby well before the war. He had very dark-brown hair, dark-brown eyes, and dark complexion. I saw him about two weeks after his return, and when I first saw him recognized him by his voice and appearance. He used to have a very peculiar stammer in his speech, which he has yet. He looks very much like he used to."

Cross-examination: "Newby had a big, thick neck, and was big around the shoulders, but was round-shouldered. He was just a big, stout man."

Mrs. Martha Lawrence: "I am a sister of William Newby's mother, and knew him from the time he was a child, living about two miles from him. He was a tolerably large man, heavy-set, with broad shoulders. He had dark complexion, dark eyes, and dark hair. He came to see me in Fairfield the fourth day after his return. I recognized him from his looks. Not a doubt on earth that this man is the identical William Newby."

Cross-examination: "There was no sandy appearance in his hair. His hair was not curly. He wore no beard, as a rule, but his beard was about the color of his hair. His neck was medium-sized for his body."

Wm. McNeely: "I served in the army with William Newby, and was intimately acquainted with him. I saw him in line of battle on Sunday morning. I went on the battleground after the battle was over, before any bodies were buried. Had heard that William Newby was killed, and searched for his body, but could not find it. I next saw him a short time after his return home, and recognized him at once. He looks very natural from chin up, but is thinner than he was in the army. I put a test to him that no one else except he and I could know. The defendant is William Newby."

Ed. Puckett: "I was well acquainted with Newby from the time we were both children. I last saw him in the army, two days before the battle of Shiloh. He was a large man, about five feet eleven inches high, and would weigh about two hundred pounds. Had dark hair, dark eyes, and a dark complexion. Saw him soon after his return in 1891, and recognized him by his countenance."

Ed. Baines, Hamilton County: "I was intimately acquainted with William Newby in the army. I was in line of battle with him on Sunday morning, and saw him after he was wounded, as we were retreating. He was lying on his right side with his head to the east, and was wounded on the left side of the head. I then thought he was dead, but had no time to stop and see. I never saw him after that until April 5, 1891. He recognized me, and I had a talk with him. Have talked with him twenty times since, and he told me things that no other people knew. I recognized him by his manner and expression of countenance and manner."

Stephen Anderson, Wayne County: "I knew William Newby before the war. He was at my house once before the war on a particular errand, and an incident occurred then. When I saw defendant he asked me about that event."

Asbury Lane: "I knew William Newby from the time we were little children until he enlisted in the army, and also served in the army with him. Saw and had a talk with him at Shiloh on the day before he was shot. He had a peculiar stoppage in his speech that I remember well. I saw him again soon after his return, and recognized him by his voice and countenance. I could see the odd expression in his eyes and features. He came to me so plain that I could not doubt it was Newby."

Henry Fetters, Fairfield: "I was in the same regiment as Newby in the army, and knew him well. I last saw him before he was shot about six o'clock Sunday morning at Shiloh. The charge that Newby was shot in was made Sunday morning, and the bodies were left on the field until Tuesday evening. I saw defendant soon after his return, and recognized him as soon as I saw his face, by the expression of his eyes, a mole near his left eye, and another on the right side of his nose. I first saw him in a buggy, and he threw up his head in a manner that was just as natural as Mr. Creighton (referring to one of the attorneys) looks now."

Wm. Colburn, Wayne County: "I served in the same regiment as William Newby in the army, and was well acquainted with him. He was a good-sized, fleshy man, with fleshy neck and face, dark hair, dark complexion, and small, dark eyes. I stood guard with him on the night of April 4, 1862, two nights before he was shot. We had a conversation that night. I saw defendant soon after he returned in 1891, and he repeated most of that conversation to me without help. I had never repeated it to anyone from the time we stood guard together until the defendant repeated it to me. Have seen the defendant several times since that. He is William Newby. From his mouth up he looks natural, although he is thin, and the back of his neck looks natural. I would have known him from appearances, and also recognized his voice."

Wm. Baity, White County: "I was in the same company as William Newby in the army, and was intimately acquainted with him. We were good friends. I stood guard with him many times. When I heard he had returned two years ago I said if it is Bill Newby he will have two moles on his face, one on the right side of the upper lip, and the other about the left temple near the eye. I distinctly remember those marks, and they came to my mind as soon as I heard of his return. I have seen him frequently since then, and found the moles as I remembered them. I was able to recognize him by his form, expression, and speech. Newby also knew circumstances connected with myself that no other but I knew. He talked them over to me."

Solomon Upton, White County, aged sixty-six: "I have been acquainted with William Newby ever since I was a boy, and enlisted in the army at the same time, but joined Company C, of the 40th Illinois. Newby was in Company D. We kept up our friendship in the army. I saw him in line of battle at Shiloh about nine o'clock Sunday morning. Saw him lying on the battle-field as we retreated, and thought he was dead, but we were retreating rapidly and I had no time to examine him. When I heard two years ago that he had come back I did not believe it, but went to see to satisfy myself, and as soon as I saw the defendant I recognized his eyes. His eyes looked like the old original Newby. He did not recognize me, and I told him my name. He said, 'Oh, yes, I know you now, and will tell you how you looked in the army,' and then told how I used to look. He is Bill Newby. There was a man in my company that looked almost like Bill, named Hiram Morris. I saw Morris in line of battle that same Sunday morning. He was reported missing after the battle, and has never been heard of since."

Capt. James Fields, Wayne County: " I was born and raised in the neighborhood where William Newby lived, and knew him well long before the war. I served in the same regiment, but in Company C. We kept up our acquaintance in the army. The last time I saw him in the service was at Shiloh, about eleven o'clock Sunday morning, in line of duty, in the first charge we made in the battle of Shiloh. That charge did not last long, and we were compelled to retreat. There were no bodies buried by our forces until late Tuesday afternoon. The bodies were then greatly swollen and had turned black, and difficult to recognize. I saw Hiram Morris in line of battle in that first charge. He was reported missing after the battle, and has never been heard from since. I am acquainted with his widow and family and know that they have never heard from him. He was about the same size as Newby, his hair, eyes, and complexion were about the same color, and in general appearance he looked much like Newby. All our regiment had on uniforms, and I think the body of Hiram Morris could easily have been mistaken for William Newby's. The defendant came to my house in February, 1891, and wanted to stay all night. After talking to me a while he said, 'I know you,' and told me my name. Have seen him frequently since then, and can see a strong resemblance to Bill Newby. He has the same peculiarities, same impediment in his speech, speaks and talks like Newby, swears like Newby used to, and has the same expression in the eyes. I have also put tests to him. From my recollection of his expression and appearance I can not doubt that the defendant is William Newby."

Cross-examination: "I think he is Newby from my recollection of how he used to look, but my belief has been strengthened by conversations with him. His looks impress me stronger than conversations."

Wm. Rose, S. L. Wallace, John Null, and Moses Robinson, of White, Wayne and Hamilton Counties, all members of the 40th Illinois Infantry, testified to knowing Hiram Morris and William Newby both in the army; that the resemblance of the two was very strong; that Morris was in line of battle at Shiloh in the first charge, and afterwards was reported missing and has never been heard from since. His family has never heard from him, but his wife has been unable to secure a pension because she could not prove his death.

Charles White, Hamilton County: "I knew Newby and his brothers before the war, and knew him in the army, being a member of the same regiment, but of Company C, and was with him up to the battle of Shiloh. I saw him about eleven o'clock Sunday morning lying on the ground, with the blood flowing from the left side of his head—dead, as I supposed. Did not stop to see if he was dead. They commenced burying the dead Tuesday evening. It was difficult to recognize the bodies of those who were killed Sunday, for it had been raining hard part of the time, and the bodies had turned black and were much swollen. I saw Hiram Morris in line of battle Sunday morning. He was missing after the battle, and has never returned. He resembled Newby, and might easily have been mistaken for him in burying the dead, especially as the bodies were in such bad condition."

George Creisle, Hamilton County: "I knew Newby well before the war. I visited him at Paducah while he was in the army. He was about five feet eleven inches tall, and had dark hair, dark-gray eyes, and dark complexion. He had a stoppage in his speech, and a very peculiar voice. I saw him soon after his return in 1891. I didn't know him at first, but did after talking to him. He has the stoppage in his speech, and same peculiar voice. I know of no man that looks more like he did thirty years ago than he does, except that he is broken down physically. This is Bill Newby. Hiram Morris and my wife were cousins. He was reported missing after the battle of Shiloh, and his wife has never heard from or of him since, and could not get a pension because she could not prove his death. Morris looked a good deal like Newby."

Newton McRill, Wayne County: "I was in same regiment as Newby in the army, and was well acquainted with him. A certain circumstance occurred when he and I were on picket together one night that other people had no opportunity to know about. I saw defendant soon after he came to White County, and he detailed that circumstance to me."

Crede A. Lay, Hamilton County: "I was a member of the 40th Regiment, and was well acquainted with Newby. I saw him in line of battle at Shiloh on Sunday morning after he was shot. One of the boys was holding his head up. There was blood all over the side of his head. I didn't think he was dead, but thought he would be in a minute or two. I said, 'Boys, he is dead, and we had better get out of here.' Some of them said 'He is not dead, but soon will be.' The battle was fought on Sunday and Monday, and the dead were buried on Tuesday afternoon. It had been raining, and was warm. The bodies were much discolored, almost as black as my hat (referring to a black woolen hat in his hand), and were badly swollen. It would be hard to tell them from black men except from their hair and their beard. It was hard to identify one's own friends. I next met him on the railroad near McLeansboro. He stopped me, and said, 'Hello, did you get crippled in the army like me?' (Witness is crippled.) I stopped and talked to him, and thought I ought to know this man, and finally it came to me that it was William Newby, who, I supposed, was dead. I examined him, and found a scar corresponding with the wound I saw on his head at Shiloh, and a mole that I remembered. I took him to a hotel, and sent word to the Newby family that Bill had returned."

Mr. Lay was later recalled, and testified that Pension Examiner Holmes had taken a statement from him. In the statement he had said that he thought Newby was dead after the battle, and saw the boys roll him over and take some tobacco and a knife out of his pocket. When asked if Newby used tobacco, he said he did not think so, but knew positively that the boys took some tobacco from the man whom they thought was William Newby.

G. J. George, Fairfield: "I knew William Newby from the time I could remember, up to the battle of Shiloh; lived near to him, and knew all of his family. I was orderly sergeant of the company Newby belonged to at the battle of Shiloh, and saw him in the line of battle Sunday morning in the first charge. He and a few other men were a little in advance of their company. At the first of the charge the captain was shot, and the men broke their line and scattered. After that there wasn't much line of battle, but companies C and D intermixed and got behind trees, stumps, and whatever protection they could. I next saw Newby by a small tree. He had been leaning against the tree, and was then falling over on his right side. There was blood on the left side of his head. I made the detail for burying the dead on Tuesday evening. The men were tired and worn out, having had no rest.since Sunday morning, and wanted to shirk the duty of burying the dead bodies until they had rested and got some sleep. The bodies were then swollen and offensive to the smell, and the burying was done hurriedly. They were dressed in uniform, and in their condition all looked alike. I could only recognize the bodies that I examined closely. I recognized two bodies, but did not see Newby's body to know it. I made the report of the killed of Company D, and gave Newby in the list of the dead. Did not know that he was killed of my own knowledge, but got the information from the men in the company. I went to see Newby the Sunday after he came back, and have frequently seen him since. I don't see how he can be anybody else, and have no doubt it is he. I have put him to such tests that I can not see how he can be anybody else but William Newby, unless one can believe in the supernatural. There was one man in the company who maintained that Newby was not killed. That was a hospital steward, a brother-in-law of Newby's. He said he had looked for Newby's body and it was not on the field. He was very positive that Newby was not killed. Newby fell about six to ten feet from Adam Files. There were eight of Company D reported killed. Seven bodies were buried where Company D had been stationed, and there was no dispute about their identity. The captain's body was taken away by his son. The next time Company D was called together, all of them were accounted for."

Marion Files, Morgan County, Mo.: "I lived in Waybe County, Ill., before the war. William Newby was my uncle. I used to trim his hair before the war, joined the same company in the army, and frequently cut his hair there. It was dark and coarse. I saw Newby in the battle of Shiloh. I was twice wounded, and was trying to get to the rear, and crawled past Newby. He was wounded in the right leg, and was trying to get up. I said, 'Bill, what's the matter?' and he said, 'I am shot all to pieces.' I think the wound was in the right thigh. I have no doubt that the defendant is Newby."

Hans Goodrich, McLeansboro: "I knew Newby well before he enlisted, also knew him in the army. I saw him in the spring of 1891, and he has stayed at my house as often as four nights since then. There is a strong resemblance to his former appearance in his eyes, forehead, and general shape of the head, also his expression. I have talked to him frequently in the last two years. Sometimes he would talk very intelligently, but at other times very much off."

Question: "Is this man William Newby?"

"That's what's left of him."

Mrs. Martha Greathouse, Arkadelphia, Ark., sister of William Newby: "I am sixty-two years old. William was about six years older than I. Lived with him until I was married, and after that we visited each other frequently. He was a large, fleshy man, weighing probably one hundred and ninety pounds. His hair was very dark brown and rather coarse, eyes yellowish black, and complexion dark. There was nothing unusual about his hands, except they were fleshy. I first learned of his return by reading of it in the papers while I was sick in Mt. Vernon, Ind. When I got able I went to Mill Shoals to see him, and did not expect to see him until I got to the house in the country, but I saw him at the depot, and recognized him. I recognized his voice, the expression of his eyes, and the peculiar stammer in his speech. This is a family peculiarity. At that time Presley Newby said it was William. I do not believe defendant is of sound mind. I say he is my brother."

Mrs. Mary Tullis, Wayne County, sister of William Newby: "I always lived close to William until he went to the war. He was a large man, about five feet ten or eleven inches tall, with dark eyes, dark complexion, and dark hair. I remember two moles on his face, one on left temple, other on right side of his upper lip. I also remember a cut he received on left foot with an axe. It was lengthwise of his foot. He was crippled a long time from it, and it left a long scar. He was also kicked on the right shin by a colt, which left a large scar. He was brought to my house soon after his return. I have talked to him in his lucid intervals, and he has told me many family affairs that occurred when we were children. He is my brother. I have no kind of doubt in the world. He resembles my folks in his motions and in his face, and has the same peculiar stoppage in his speech that he had be-before the war, which is a family characteristic. He looks like he did before the war except he is older. His voice is the same, but not so strong."

Whaley Newby: " I am a brother of William Newby. He is about twelve years older than I am. I enlisted and served in the same company as he did. I saw him Sunday morning in line of battle at Shiloh. I was wounded in the battle and did not know what became of Bill except what I was told. When we heard that he had returned about the first of April, 1891, I went with Ki Newby and young Tullis after him, and found him about seven miles below Carmi. His mind seemed to be all torn up. He was very ragged, had a beard, and looked like a tramp. I did not go clear back home with him, but went to see him the next Sunday, and talked to him. I have seen and talked to him very often since then. He is my brother William."

Mrs. Ferebe Newby, wife of William Newby: " I am the wife of William Newby. We were married in October, 1849, and settled on a tract of timber-land in White County, Ill., and cleared it out and made a farm. We had six children: Henrietta, aged forty-two; John W., forty; William, thirty-eight; Marion, thirty-six; Hezekiah, thirty-four; and Rebecca, who was three months old when her father joined the army. I heard from him up to the battle of Shiloh in 1862, and was then informed that he had been killed in that battle. I applied for a pension, and received one. I went to Texas in 1890 to live with my son John, and took up a land claim. In the early part of 1891 I received word that my husband had returned home. I went back to White County, and when I got there I first saw William at the gate of his brother Whaley Newby's house, and recognized him as soon as I looked at him. He was excited and his mind was in bad condition, and I did not talk to him much then. He always had a peculiar way of calling my name, and when he saw me the first time after his return he called my name in that same old way. In the last two years we have often talked of our married life before the war, and I know that he is my husband. Sometimes he is very crazy, and does not even know me— at other times he seems lucid. His mind is greatly improved in the past two years. As soon as I got home I gave up my pension papers, and refused to receive it any longer. I took my husband to Texas in October, 1891. He came back to Illinois to make proof of his pension papers, and I staid in Texas to hold my land claim. I saw in a paper this spring that he had been arrested, and at once started home."

Mrs. Rebecca Newby, mother of William Newby, aged ninety-five: "I am William Newby's mother. He lived with me until he was grown, and after he was married lived close to me. He was a big man, with dark-brown hair and dark skin. I am nearly blind, but have talked to William since his return, and know it is he. William had a ginger-bread birthmark about the size of my little finger-nail when he was a baby, but outgrew it."

Mrs. Newby was, of course, feeble, and was not examined at much length.

Hezekiah Newby: "I am a son of William and Ferebe Newby, and am thirty-four years old. I do not remember my father before he went to the war. I was told by Charles White, of McLeansboro, Ill., in April, 1891, that my father had come back and was at the White County poorfarm. I went to my uncle, Presley Newby, told him what I had heard, and asked him how I could tell whether he was my father or not. He said that if the man was my father I would find a long scar on his left foot, a big scar on his shin, and a mole on the right side of his upper lip. I went to see the man, and found the scars and mole as Uncle Pres had described to me. I then went to McLeansboro, and told what I had done. My uncle Presley Newby and John Files then went to the poorfarm to see the man, but when we got there found that he had left the poorfarm and started toward the Indiana line. We overtook him about seven miles below Carmi, near the Wabash River, and tried to persuade him to return to his old home. I told him that I was his son, and that he was Bill Newby. The man acted kind of dazed, crazy-like, crying and wailing, and displaying evidences of insanity. John Files and I questioned him. The defendant said his name was Bill Newby, and that Carroll Newby was his father. John Files, who had known him before he left for the war, was somewhat dazed at this statement, as he was sure it was Bill Newby, and I took him home, some sixteen miles. When we got him home the news spread that Bill Newby had returned, and his old friends came in and stood around and talked to him, several coming every day for a good while."

Several other relatives of Newby, and many more old army comrades, friends, and neighbors, testified positively that they recognized the defendant as William Newby.

One of the most interesting branches of the entire case is the testimony of seven witnesses who recognized the defendant as a character they knew in Andersonville prison in 1864 and 1865. None of these seven witnesses knew William Newby before or during the war, and, of course, could not identify the claimant as William Newby, but only knew him as a prisoner in Andersonville.

Wm. Snyder, Parkersburg, Ill.: "I was in Company H, 14th Illinois Cavalry, in the late war, and was captured by the Confederate army on Stoneman's raid July 27, 1864, and was taken to Andersonville prison about four days later. I remained there about three months, and was then taken to Florence, Ala., where I was paroled. I saw the defendant in Andersonville prison soon after I got there. He was held as a prisoner and was known as 'Crazy Jack.' The lower part of his limbs were rotten with the scurvy and gangrene sores, and he was covered with vermin. He had hardly any clothes, sometimes wore none at all, and never wore a hat. The flies and vermin would get into the sores on his legs, and he would get into the dirty water to keep them off him. I have seen the boys drag him out of the water many times, and have done it myself. I saw what was known then as the Christian Band take 'Crazy Jack' one time and bathe him and cut his hair. When they cut his hair I saw the large scar on the left side of his head. 'Crazy Jack' was a mere skeleton when I knew him in the prison. He occupied a hole in the sand twenty-five or thirty steps from my quarters, and I saw him very often, oftener than once a day. I never knew him by any other name than 'Crazy Jack.' As soon as I saw the defendant about two years ago I recognized him. I would have known him any place in the world. He was in Andersonville when I was taken away."

Mr. Snyder was later recalled, and said that "Crazy Jack," while in Andersonville, was about thirty-five to forty years old.

Joseph Russell, Carmi, Ill.: "I was a member of the 48th Illinois Infantry. I was captured by the Confederates, and taken to Andersonville prison. I got to Andersonville May 26, 1864, and remained there about three months. I knew a man there called 'Crazy Jack' very well, and as soon as I saw defendant in Carmi about two years ago I recognized him as 'Crazy Jack.' When I first saw him in 1891 I was standing in my store door at Carmi, and saw him coming down the street with some other people. He was off some distance, and as soon as I caught sight of him I said to a man I was talking to, 'If that ain't "Crazy Jack," by Jingo, it's his ghost,' and when he came closer I said, 'It's "Crazy Jack" and there's no rubbing it out.' This man is 'Crazy Jack.'"

Henry Jamison, Wayne County: "I enlisted in the army at Shawneetown, Ill., and was in the 56th Illinois Infantry. I was captured, taken prisoner, and taken to Andersonville prison in October, 1864, and remained there until April

16, 1865. I knew the defendant in Andersonville as 'Crazy Jack.' He was then in a fearful condition. His lower limbs were all black and broken out with running sores. He was still in Andersonville when I left there. I recognized the defendant as 'Crazy Jack.' Knew him by his eyes, expression, and his walk. He walks now like he did then, but a little better. We regarded him as very crazy at Andersonville."

Job Downey: "I belonged to Company D, 29th Infantry. I was captured and taken to Andersonville prison by the Confederates in May, 1864. I stayed there that time until about the last of August or the first of September, and was then removed, but was returned in the winter. I saw the defendant a great many times during my first confinement in the prison, but was given quarters in another part of the prison the second time. I often saw him up and down the branch. I thought he had about as much sense as a hog. I recognize the defendant by his eyes, the shape of his head, his general condition, and his walk. I recognized him before I talked to him by his walk, by the picture I had in my mind of him when he was in Andersonville. I have conversed with the defendant, and he has told me incidents that occurred in

Andersonville while we were prisoners there. In addition to these witness, Emanuel Berry, of Carmi, and Uriah King and James Grant, both of Springfield, testified that they were prisoners at Andersonville, knew "Crazy Jack" there and identified defendant as him. They said that he was at that time aged about thirty-five to forty.

D. F. Morgan and George McIntosh both testified to having seen defendant fall off a road-cart under the horse he was driving in the summer of 1891. He was rigid and frothing at the mouth. They pulled him out from under the horse, and he recovered in a little while.

The defense had the evidence of one man who had seen "Rickety Dan," of Tennessee, and who testified that claimant was not that man—Nathan Reid, Wayne County: "I was employed in business in Tennessee. My health had been poor, and my physicians thought a change of climate would benefit me. For that reason I took a position as traveling agent for Dr. Champion's medicines, and traveled through the country in a buggy. I was in Tennessee all through July, 1869. I saw a queer character close to Linville, Tenn., which I think is about fifty miles from Nashville, who was called 'Rickety Dan.' I stayed all night at the same farmhouse once. He was peddling cheap jewelry. The proprietor told me that he was 'Rickety Dan,' and I think, but am not positive about the last name, that he said 'Rickety Dan' Benton. I saw him as often as four times. The defendant is not that man. 'Rickety Dan' was not so tall as defendant by two or three inches. The defendant walked like him, but better."

The last branch of the evidence taken up by the defense was the expert testimony. It was very interesting, and, the author thought, of great importance.

Dr. C. W. Sibley, of Fairfield: "I am a practicing physician and surgeon. Am a graduate of Bellevue Hospital College, and have been practicing twenty-five years. I have examined the defendant four or five times as a member of the pension board at Fairfield. I found no indication of rickets. The defendant never had the rickets. If the defendant ever had the rickets it could be told now. I have examined the scar on defendant's head. It is a place where, if it injured the brain, would cause the defendant to walk as he does. A blow might cause an indentation of the inner table of the skull without external indentation. A blow on the head in such a case might produce blood-clot; a clot might be followed by paresis, insanity, epilepsy, or a condition of the nervous system known as neurosis. The defendant has some indications of epilepsy, particularly scars on his tongue, as if from biting it. The wound might have been made by a projectile, such as a ball or a part of a shell. The defendant's mind is not right at any time, and he is in the condition known as dementia. This condition may have been caused by injury to the brain. The scar on the defendant's thigh is the scar from a gunshot wound. I saw the scar on the inside of his left foot. It was caused by some sharp instrument. I also found the scar on the shin. It is the result of an ulcer, and may have been caused by a bruise, such as the kick of a horse. The defendant was not a cripple until he was nearly grown. I have examined him and find his bones all fully and perfectly developed. The wound on the head is in such a location that it would affect the nerves of limbs on the opposite side of the body, and cause the lack of control of the limbs and the peculiar gait the defendant has. In injuries to the brain of that kind which affect the nerves of the body the opposite side of the body is affected. Such a condition as the defendant's would weaken the memory, and make the subject incapable of sustained mental effort. Such condition might be permanent, but in case of blood-clot it might be absorbed, and in pressure from displacement of the skull the bones might adjust themselves. After ten or fifteen years in this condition no change would be likely to take place for the better. The mental condition of the patient may be affected by extraneous circumstances."

Dr. J. N. Dixon, Dr. E. S. Fowler, Dr. E. P. Bartlett, of the Springfield pension board, and Dr. I. S. Hughes, of the pension board, all of Springfield, and Dr. C. C. Truscott, Cisne, Ill., Dr. Chester Files, of Bone Gap, Ill., and Dr. Hunter, Springfield, Ill., all testified that they had made careful examinations of the defendant, and said that the defendant had never had rickets, could not have been crippled from birth or early childhood, and that his mental condition and his peculiar gait were caused from the wound on the head, which had injured his brain. They said the same as Dr. Sibley in regard to the scar on the defendant's lower limbs and foot. They also said that there were signs that defendant was subject to epilepsy, indicated by scars on his tongue, where he had probably bitten himself.

The defense closed its case here, and District Attorney Shutt announced that the government would introduce some evidence in rebuttal.

REBUTTAL.

Silas Biggerstaff, Hamilton County, Ill., was the first witness called in rebuttal, and said: "I knew William Newby before the war. I first saw the defendant some time in March, 1891, before he was taken to the home of the Newbys. He came to my house, and staid some time. He said his name was Allen Newby. He talked about William Newby, and where William Newby was killed, with a John Simpson, in my presence. Simpson told him that William Newby was killed at Shiloh, and they talked about that for about half an hour. Defendant never once claimed to be William Newby. He said that he was in the battle of Shiloh, and was wounded in the leg in the first charge, and when the rebels drove the Union troops back he asked a rebel soldier for a drink of water, and the soldier struck him on the side of the head with the butt end of his gun. Defendant said he had a brother at Mill Shoals. He was a puzzle to me because he talked so rambling, and told so many unreasonable tales."

A. A. Holmes, Sullivan, Ind., a former special examiner, who worked on the claimant's pension application for some time, was then called and read two sworn statements of the defendant; one taken in January, 1892, and the other taken January 4, 1893.

The defense objected to the reading of the statements in rebuttal upon the ground that the defendant had not gone upon the stand, but the court held that insanity was one of the defenses made by the defendant's attorneys, and therefore it would be proper to admit the statements to show the condition of defendant's mind. The statements contained nearly two hundred pages of closely written legal cap. In them the defendant undertook to give a detailed account of his whereabouts from the time he was in Andersonville prison until he reached White County in 1891. The statements did not agree in many respects, and contained many unreasonable stories, but showed that he had been in various poorhouses throughout Ohio, Indiana, Kentucky, and Illinois, under the name of Daniel Benton —also in the Tennessee state penitentiary. The statements showed the defendant to be a man of rambling mind, but yet a remarkable memory. To undertake to give their contents would be to tire the reader out, and would throw no light on the case.

W. H. Merritt, recalled by the prosecution: "I was back in the hospital during the battle of Shiloh. No, I was not wounded, but helped a wounded man to the hospital, and staid there. The Confederates captured the hospital while I was in it. When the Union troops were about to retake the hospital the Confederates called on everybody who could walk to go with them. I laid still, and did not go. It was about fifteen miles to the nearest railroad station, Corinth. The wounded were left on the field and in the hospital until after the battle was over. I think the Confederate army took a large number of wounded men prisoners, but I did not know of them taking away any prisoners who could not walk. The rebels took no prisoners after Sunday."

Capt. W. S. Campbell, of the adjutant general's office of this state, was put upon the stand. He brought a copy of the record of the companies of the 40th Infantry, and was asked to read the record of Hiram Morris, of Company C. Objection was raised on the ground that this was not the original record, but it was claimed by the prosecution that it was competent as it was published by the government authority. The court ruled that the evidence was admissible at whatever value it should prove to possess.

"Hiram Morris, private, twenty-two years of age, six feet two inches high, black hair, black eyes, dark complexion; farmer; a resident of Berry, Pike County, Ill.; entered August 26, 1861, discharged for disability April 13, 1863."

I have been in the adjutant general's office about three months and have found about a half a dozen mistakes in these reports.

There was another Morris, Jeremiah Morris, of whom no record is preserved as to what became of him. There are about thirty members of the company of whom no final record is made. Mr. Campbell was asked to turn to Company D, and found the name of William Newby. There was no record as to what became of him. The date of his enlistment is August 8, 1861, and he is described as being five feet eleven inches high, with dark hair and gray eyes, and dark complexion.

Dr. B. M. Griffith, of Springfield: "I know the disease, Friedrich's ataxia. It is considered hereditary. Sometimes it develops in childhood and sometimes later in life. It is called ataxia because of the peculiar motions of those afflicted with it. It affects the brain as well as the spinal cord, and does not affect the nutrition or development. Locomotor ataxia is the result of slow inflammation of the cord, or where it is caused by a blow on the head, produced by extravasated blood or pressure from depression of the skull, produces progressive paralysis. One foot would not be larger than another. Friedrich's ataxia would produce atrophy and apparent deformity. He illustrated by the copy of the examination of William Newby by the Fairfield pension examiners and diagrams of the patient's feet in which the feet are unsymmetrical. This is never produced by locomotor ataxia. This condition can not be produced by a blow on the head in manhood. From the walk of the defendant, believe he has Friedrich's ataxia. He is knock-kneed, his feet turn sidewise, and he has the peculiar rolling motion of the eyeballs which is characteristic of Friedrich's ataxia. I have only seen the defendant on the street and sitting in the court-room. I could tell whether he has locomotor ataxia or Friedrich's ataxia if I made an examination of him. Any competent physician could do so. The defendant has not got the rickets."

Dr. T. W. Dresser, of Springfield, testified substantially the same as Dr. Griffith.

Dr. C. W. Sibley was then recalled, and said that the diagram referred to above was not pretended to be accurate in size, but was made simply to show how the defendant's foot was twisted and deformed. In fact, the defendant's feet are of the same size. The diagram was then offered in evidence by the prosecution. This was objected to by the defense unless the whole report of the Fairfield pension board was allowed to go with it. The court overruled the objection and allowed the one page of the report without the balance to go to the jury.

Thomas H. McBride, Cincinnati, Ohio, special pension examiner: "I took the defendant from Mill Shoals to Tennessee in April of this year. We went from Mill Shoals to Flora, Ill., from Flora to Louisville, from Louisville to Nashville, where we staid a day, and drove from there to Brentwood, Tenn. On the way from Louisville to Nashville the defendant wanted to read, and I allowed him to pick out a book, which he read on the train. In Nashville, on the road to Brentwood and in that neighborhood we saw a good many people who recognized the defendant as 'Rickety Dan.' On the way to Andrew Wooten's house we came to a long lane, at the end of which there was a house. Up the road, about the same distance, was another house. I did not know which was Wooten's house, and said to defendant, 'Now, Dan, you know all about this country; tell me which house Wooten lives in, and don't make me drive through this mud to the wrong house.' Defendant said, 'I don't know where he lives, but I guess we had better drive up the lane.' We drove up there, and found Wooten. When Wooten came out defendant said, 'Hallo, have your two brothers-in-law got out of the penitentiary yet?' I asked Wooten if he knew the defendant. He said he thought he did, but asked me to have him get out and walk and he could tell me. I had the defendant get out and walk, and Wooten then said, 'He is "Rickety Dan" Benton.' Defendant then claimed that he did not know Wooten. When we got to Lem Sawyer's house the defendant called out to Sawyer, 'Come, take me back to the penitentiary,' but then pretended not to know Sawyer. When Sawyer told the defendant that he had never taken but one man to the penitentiary and that was Dan Benton, and said, 'You are the man,' the defendant replied, 'You can have your way down here, but I have got four counties back of me up in Illinois, and I am going to get a twenty-thousand-dollar pension.' He also told Mrs. McDowell, who was trying to fool him, that he knew he was Dan Benton, and when she asked him why he tried to deny his name, he said that he was suing the government for a big pension, and could not give himself away. The defendant would pretend not to know the different people down there, but I could see the look of recognition in his eye every time. The defendant is a man of remarkable memory and of low cunning, but not shrewd."

Mr. McBride was the last witness placed upon the stand. His testimony, which was finished on Thursday evening, July 20, concluded the evidence, which had consumed more than eight days. At the close of his evidence the court adjourned until 8:30 o'clock the next morning, at which time the argument would be commenced.

The well-known ability of the attorneys who were to make the arguments in this most remarkable of cases caused an immense throng to be in the Federal court-room the next morning.

Mr. Drennen made the opening argument for the prosecution in a most masterly effort of three hours. He was followed by Col. Johns, Judge Kramer, and Mr. Creighton, in forcible and eloquent speeches for the defense. Mr. Shutt, in a strong effort, closed the case for the government.

At the conclusion of the arguments the judge gave the instructions to the jury, which are found elsewhere.

When Judge Allen had finished reading his charge it was handed to the foreman of the jury, together with the statements of the defendant read by Mr. Holmes, and the other documentary evidence that had been offered for the consideration of the jury during the trial, and at 2:07 o'clock the twelve jurymen, in charge of two officers, retired to consider the case. The defendant took the arm of the woman who believes him to be her husband, and who has been so faithful to him, and with his peculiar gait hobbled out of the room. The attorneys and large audience also left, and in five minutes the courtroom, which had been packed with people for the past two weeks, was vacated except by the officers of the court and two or three lawyers who had another case to take up.

There was a surprised silence when eighteen

minutes later, at 2:25, the bailiff announced that the jury had reached an agreement. Proceedings were suspended, and the jury came in. The defendant was now wanted. It took a bailiff twenty minutes to find him. At 2:45 he came shambling in, followed by Ki Newby. It took ten minutes to get the lawyers together, and then the verdict was read. It was:

"We, the jury, find the defendant guilty."

Surprise was written on every face in the court-room. Everybody looked at "Rickety Dan" Benton, but he did not seem to care, for he only fanned a little harder with his old wool hat and looked a trifle harder at the floor. Mrs. Newby was not present. When the news reached her she broke into tears. The Court proceeded with another case. The defendant remained in the court-room half an hour. Then a deputy marshal took charge of him, and the last seen of him he was tottering up the street leaning on the arm of the officer.

The defendant's attorneys informed the Court that they would ask for a new trial, and were given until the next Tuesday to formally enter the motion.

There was intense excitement on the street when the result became known. The walks became crowded with people excitedly discussing the verdict. At the close of the trial it was the opinion of a vast majority of those who had listened to the evidence day after day that the defendant would be acquitted.

Money was freely offered by the people to pay the expense of a new trial if granted by Judge Allen, and if refused, for an appeal to the Supreme Court of the United States. On Wednesday, July 26, the attorneys for claimant filed a written motion for a new trial, alleging that—

First, the verdict was contrary to the evidence.

Second, the verdict was contrary to the law.

Third, the verdict was contrary to the law and evidence.

Fourth, certain members of the jury had formed and expressed an opinion of the guilt of the defendant before being accepted as jurors.

Fifth, certain members of the jury had formed and expressed an opinion of the guilt of defendant during the trial.

Sixth, other misconduct of the jury.

Seventh, the Court admitted improper evidence for the prosecution.

Eighth, the Court refused competent evidence offered by the defense.

Ninth, the Court in its charge to the jury erred as to the law.

Tenth, the Court in its charge improperly discussed the evidence.

Eleventh, newly discovered evidence.

Twelfth, other good and sufficient reasons.

The Court then set August 14 as the date for arguing the above motion. On that date defendant's attorneys filed eight affidavits of persons who had known the original "Rickety Dan" Benton, describing him as having very light hair, deep-blue eyes, pug nose, deeply sunken between the eyes, and affected with the rickets.

There were also affidavits presented by different people who had heard three members of the jury express opinions of the guilt of the claimant before and during the trial.

The district attorney then asked until August 26 to make reply to those affidavits, which was granted, and that day set for the formal argument of the motion for a new trial.

On the 26th and 27th lengthy arguments were made for a new trial by Mr. Creighton, Col. Johns, and Gen. McCartney, of Chicago, Ex-Attorney General of Illinois, who had proffered his services to the defendant.

More affidavits regarding the expression of prejudice against the defendant by one of the jurymen made before the trial, and eight more affidavits of persons who had seen Dan Benton in 1892 were offered, but the Court refused to allow them filed, saying that it had announced on the 14th of August that no affidavits would be received after that date. At the conclusion of the arguments the Court overruled the motion for a new trial, and sentenced the prisoner to hard labor in the penitentiary for two years.

Defendant's attorneys, as a last resort, prayed an appeal, which was allowed upon the defendant giving, within sixty days, a bond in the sum of one thousand dollars to secure the costs.

On the 30th day of August William Newby, or Daniel Benton, whichever he may be, was taken from the Sangamon County jail to Chester, Ill., where he was placed in the penitentiary to serve his sentence.

Thus ended the trial, so far as this narration is concerned, of one of the strangest and most remarkable cases in the history of jurisprudence, a case which will undoubtedly be discussed in the law-books of all nations, and take a prominent place among the *causes célèbre*.

Meanwhile the claimant is serving his sentence in the penitentiary, and his attorneys and friends are using every effort to raise sufficient means to take his case to the highest tribunal of the land.

HON. JAMES M'CARTNEY.

LETTER FROM HON. JAMES McCARTNEY, EX-ATTORNEY GENERAL OF ILLINOIS.

Unity Building,
Chicago, September 4, 1893.

Capt. G. J. George, Fairfield, Ill.

Dear Friend: Your favor of the 1st inst. received, asking a statement of the substance of the objections to Judge Allen's charge to the jury in the Newby case, and his answer thereto in overruling the motion for a new trial.

The principal objections we made to the judge's charge to the jury were: The statement to the jury that they might consider and pass upon the expert evidence in the light of their "common sense and experience in life."

We contended that this instruction was wrong, for the reason that the sole ground for the introduction of expert evidence was that the jury were not supposed to know or have any experience concerning the subject upon which the evidence was offered. In this case the expert evidence was offered to show, as the judge says, " whether defendant is suffering from hereditary or acquired disease "; in other words, whether the defendant had rickets, or was suffering from wounds. The jury were told, in short, that they could believe the physicians or not, according as their " common sense and experience in life " told them, whether it was rickets or wounds in the head that affected the defendant. In passing upon the motion the judge in no way or manner referred to, or passed upon, this objection.

The next principal objection we offered to the charge was that the judge instructed the jury upon the question of insanity, that, " if the defendant at the time of the application was an idiot, a lunatic, or affected with insanity, he should be acquitted."

The law on this question is as laid down in the cases of Chase *vs.* The People, 40 Ill. 352, and Dacey *vs.* The People, 116 Ill. 573, that if insanity is alleged in defense, and there is sufficient evidence to raise a reasonable doubt, it devolves upon the prosecution to prove the defendant's sanity beyond a reasonable doubt. The judge left this all out of his charge to the jury, and left it for the jury to understand that if they simply *believed* that the defendant had sufficient mind to know right from wrong they should find him guilty.

The Judge, in overruling the motion for a new trial, said on this point that he thought the general charge at the conclusion, saying "that before you can convict him, the evidence must, in your opinion, establish his guilt beyond a reasonable doubt," covered the question of the defendant's sanity.

The next objection was the statement to the jury by the Judge that "the doubt, however, must be a reasonable one, arising out of the unsatisfactory character of the government's evidence." This, we contended, told the jury, in substance, that they must found their doubts on the government's evidence alone. If *that* satisfied them beyond a reasonable doubt it made no difference what evidence was introduced in defense, they might convict. Of course, such is not the law.

Judge Allen answered this by saying that he thought the jury could not be misled by this because, in the conclusion, he said "if from the entire evidence you have an abiding conviction of the truth of the charge, then you should find him guilty."

But this last clause of his charge we object to, also, for the reason that the words "abiding conviction" mean only a permanent or established belief, and the Judge should have added the other words always used in defining a reasonable doubt, to wit, "*to a moral certainty*," making the proper instruction read, " if from the entire evidence you have an abiding conviction *to a moral certainty* of the truth of the charge, then you should find him guilty."

We finally, after making several minor objections to various other portions of the charge, made the general objection that the whole charge, from the first sentence, in which he calls the defendant Daniel Benton, to the last sentence, in which he directs the jury to find the defendant "simply guilty or not guilty," gave the jury clearly to understand that the Judge believed the defendant to be Daniel Benton instead of William Newby, and that the jury so believing, and to save themselves the trouble of trying to reconcile the conflicting evidence, took the easier way of agreeing upon a verdict, in accordance with the wishes of the Judge.

In answer to this, Judge Allen said, in substance, that the Supreme Court, in two instances at least, had held that a federal judge had the right to instruct the jury upon the facts in the case, and to give his opinion thereon, and might give his opinion of the guilt or innocence of the defendant if he gave the jury to understand that they were the judges of the evidence.

In this we think the Judge enlarged too greatly the meaning of the language of the Supreme Court in the cases he no doubt referred to. One of the cases referred to by the Judge is probably the case of Lovejoy *vs.* U. S., 128 U. S. Sup. Ct. Rep., p. 171, in which the court, by Mr. Justice Gray, says: " It is established by repeated decisions that a court of the United States, in submitting a case, may, at its discretion, express its opinion upon the facts, and that such an opinion is not reviewable on error so long as no rule of law is incorrectly stated and all matters of fact are ultimately submitted to the determination of the jury." The same Judge stated the rule almost in the same words in the case of The Vicksburg & Meridian R. R. Co. *vs.* Putnam, 118 U. S. Sup. Ct. Rep., p. 545.

In neither of these cases did the court pretend to draw or form a conclusion from the evidence, and intimate such conclusion to the jury. In the first case cited, the question at issue was whether or not the names of the sureties on a bond were forged. The Judge said, "As to the signature of Thomas W. Means, I think you may have some difficulty in finding that it was a forgery. Of course it is not my place to express an opinion, or say whether or not I think it is genuine. All I say is that you must examine the matter carefully and fully, and weigh all the testimony that bears upon the subject, and if you can say that his signature is a forgery it is for you to do so." This is the whole of the instruction, or charge, complained of upon which was founded the decision of Mr. Justice Gray.

How different from this was Judge Allen's charge. After raising all possible doubts as to the truth, honesty, sincerity, and knowledge of facts sworn to by defendant's witnesses, without a hint that possibly any of the government's witnesses might be mistaken in anything they had sworn to, the Judge merely said: "But, gentlemen, I forbear any general discussion of this evidence. In this country the evidence goes directly from the witness to the jury. The court's duty is performed when all proper aid is attempted to be given in assisting the jury in applying or placing value upon certain of its phases, which, by reason of want of familiarity with rules in regard to evidence, they are not able to readily and satisfactorily dispose of."

Did it aid the jury in placing value upon the phases of the evidence for want of familiarity with its rules by insinuating to them that evidence of defendant's witnesses "often wholly unreliable" when they reached their conclusion that he was Newby from conversations and "tests they had applied to him"? Or that mere opinions of defendant's witnesses that he was Newby was of doubtful value when "they had not seen the party for thirty years"? Or that it is "remarkable that there is an entire absence of evidence either that the Confederates removed prisoners captured at Shiloh who could not walk or of the class to which the seriously wounded Newby belonged, or that any other prisoner captured by them at that battle ever found his way into the Andersonville prison," etc., etc., every sentence in the charge raising some doubt of defendant's innocence and leaving the matter of his guilt unquestioned?

In the case of the Chesapeake & Ohio Canal *vs.* Knapp, 9 Peters, U. S. Sup. Ct. Rep., p. 541, Mr. Justice McLean, for the Supreme Court, said, "Where there is evidence on the point, the court may be called on to instruct the jury as to the law, but it is for them to determine on the effect of the evidence."

And in Tracy *vs.* Swarthout, 10 Peters, U. S. Sup. Ct. Rep., p. 80, the same Judge says, "A court may not only present the facts proved in their charge to the jury, but give their opinion as to those facts for the consideration of the jury. But, as the jurors are the triers of facts, such an expression of opinion by the court should be so guarded as to leave the jury free in the exercise of their own judgments. They should be made to distinctly understand that the instruction was not given as a point of law, by which they were to be governed, but as a mere opinion as to the facts, and to which they should give no more weight than it was entitled to."

In the case of McLanahan *vs.* Universal Ins. Co., 1 Peters, U. S. Sup. Ct. Rep., p. 170, Mr. Justice Story, for the Supreme Court, said, "It is doubtless within the province of a court, in the exercise of its discretion, to sum up the facts in the case to the jury and submit them, with the inferences of law deducible therefrom, to the free judgment of the jury. But care should be taken in all such cases to separate the law from the facts, and to leave the latter in unequivocal terms to the jury as their true and peculiar province."

Tested by these authorities I can not see how it can possibly be claimed that Judge Allen's charge to the jury can be sustained. He did not guard his opinions by in any way indicating to the jury that they were not to be governed by his opinions. He did not separate the law from the facts. He did not submit the facts to the free judgment of the jury.

After Judge Allen overruled the motion for a new trial we filed a motion in arrest of the judgment, one ground of which is unquestionably a good one for the arrest. According to the indictment the defendant is Daniel Benton, and as such he attempted to defraud the United States Government by representing himself to be William Newby, demanded a pension, and in his application alleged that he had never been discharged from the United States service, and was still a soldier in its army. Everyone knows that no person but a *discharged* soldier or sailor is entitled to a pension. This application could therefore deceive or defraud no one. The law under which this indictment was found declares that any person making any claim upon the government, or any department thereof, knowing such claim to be false shall be punished, etc. This application, on its face, proved that it was no claim upon the government. Consequently the charge could in no event be sustained.

The foregoing is all written upon the legal questions in the case. Of course, our main, principal, and never-to-be-lost-sight-of ground of defense is that the defendant is William Newby and not Daniel Benton. Were it not that we fully, conscientiously, and undoubtedly believe the defendant to be William Newby, and that on another trial we will prove this so conclusively that even Judge Allen will admit it, we would not urge these technical objections to the former trial. But believing that he is William Newby, and believing that we will so prove him to be, and that he has not had a fair and impartial trial, we intend to use all the lawful means in our power to secure another and fairer trial for him through the Supreme Court of the United States. Your Friend,

JAMES MCCARTNEY

WILLIAM NEWBY RECEIVING HIS SENTENCE
FROM JUDGE JOSHUA ALLEN.

"If you are William Newby you are a very unfortunate and a greatly injured man. If you are Daniel Benton you are a very guilty man. The jury has said that you are Daniel Benton, and with that verdict I have expressed my satisfaction.

"The Court, in the discharge of his duty in connection with this case, sentences you to two years imprisonment at Chester at hard labor."

CHAPTER X.

THE COURT'S INSTRUCTIONS TO THE JURY.

THE defendant, Daniel Benton, *alias* William Newby, was indicted by the Grand Jury at the present term of the Court for presenting a false pension claim against the government, in which it is alleged he falsely claimed to have been the identical William Newby who enlisted in the service of the government of the United States in the war of the rebellion on August 6, 1861, and becoming a member of Company D, in the 40th Regiment Illinois Infantry Volunteers, and receiving, as he states in his application, a wound on the head at the battle of Shiloh on April 6, 1862. The indictment charges that the defendant is not the said William Newby who belonged to said company and regiment and who was so wounded, but, on the contrary, is Daniel Benton, who was not a soldier. The case is an important one. The government during and after the war, through the several acts of congress on that subject, justly and liberally provided for pensioning soldiers suffering under disabilities for wounds or diseases contracted and incurred during their service, but properly devising severe penalties against anyone who should falsely and fraudulently attempt to draw money from the national treasury without having performed military service. This legislation should be construed and carried out so as to encourage applications for pensions of meritorious soldiers, but at the same time defeat all fraudulent applications, and punish such as incur its penalties. This case, for some reasons, seems to have aroused intense feeling in many portions of the district, a feeling more intense on the streets and in the court-house than I have observed since coming on the bench. Such manifestations do not have a healthy look, and there is certainly no occasion for them. It is preposterous to assume that any other motive than an honest desire to discharge official duties actuated the officers of the government in investigating defendant's case, and accordingly they brought the trial under safeguards and forms of law. You also will, I am sure, in rendering your verdict, be governed by your love of government under the law and evidence.

One of the questions with which you have to deal is that of identity—the identity of two persons, in fact—William Newby and Daniel Benton. Experience has shown that this question is frequently one of difficulty, and there are complications in this demanding your highest inteligence. Many witnesses have sworn that the defendant is the identical William Newby he claims to be in his pension application. Many others have sworn that he is not—that he is Daniel Benton, who, born in White County, Ill., and when only a few years old, in company with his mother, moved with Andrew Wooten, in 1848 or 1849, to Williamson County, Tenn., where he remained until 1862 or 1863.

In determining which of these two classes, or bodies, of witnesses is most reliable you should in the first place carefully comprehend the traits and characteristics of the two men, socially, morally, and mentally. The resemblance of one man to another physically often misleads, but the old aphorism that no two men were ever alike within is full of wisdom for your guidance. Of the class of witnesses testifying that defendant is Newby many reach that conclusion because of conversations had with him, and "tests," to use their language, they had applied to him, the inference being that such conversations and tests related to matters of which the witness and Newby were severally cognizant. Such testimony is often unreliable. The man such witnesses call Newby may have been informed of such circumstances and equipped for such tests. It may be true, also, that many of this class of witnesses, without consideration, and from sympathy, or the charm of mystery, hastily formed, or thought they did, the opinion that defendant was Newby, and afterwards regarded him with no suspicion, and gradually, but naturally, accepted his narrations without any attempt to ascertain whether they were truthful or unreasonable.

But, gentlemen, you are the judges of the evidence, and in view of your experience in life, and your knowledge of men and things, must pass upon the value of their opinions on the question of identity expressed by witnesses when it is admitted that they had not seen the party for thirty years. A number of witnesses professing to identify defendant as Newby testified to having seen him in line of battle at Shiloh on April 6, 1862. Some say he was, as they thought, mortally wounded; others that he was killed, and buried in a common grave, with six or seven comrades, on the battlefield.

The entire theory of the defense is that on that occasion Newby was very severely wounded, and captured by the Confederates as a prisoner of war, and removed by them several hundred miles to Andersonville, Ga., where he pined for two or three years in prison, and afterwards in some manner found his way to the poorhouses in Ohio, Indiana, Kentucky, and Tennessee, and afterwards to the penitentiary of the latter state. It may occur to some of you as remarkable that there is an entire absence of evidence offered that the Confederates removed prisoners captured at Shiloh who could not walk, or the class to which Newby belonged, or that any other prisoner captured by them at that battle of his class ever found his way into Andersonville prison.

In examining into the theories of the government and defense, certain facts may be regarded as conceded. Among these, by the defense, that the man identified by the witnesses as having been in Andersonville prison in 1864, called "Crazy Jack," and afterwards in the Ohio poorhouse in 1869, in the Indiana and Kentucky poorhouses in 1871, '72, '73, and '74, and afterwards sentenced to the penitentiary in Tennessee in 1877, as the present defendant. And this forces the inquiry as to whether differences in appearance and conduct, if any have been shown by the evidence, have been satisfactorily explained or accounted for; for instance, is it reasonable or rational to believe that one who manifests the judgment or strength of mind the witnesses abscribe to defendant in Ohio, Indiana, Kentucky, and Tennessee, from 1869 to 1889, would have been entirely and utterly forgotten to his old home, family, and friends?

Considerations of this character demand your conscientious, intelligent attention. You have observed how members of the Newby family differ on the question of identity, two brothers and one sister saying that defendant is not Newby; and two sisters and one brother giving as their opinion that he is their brother. The wife of William Newby is also permitted, under the peculiar circumstances of the case, of testifying, but you are instructed, in passing on the evidence, to keep in mind the fact that her testimony was given under belief that defendant was her husband, and for which she had mourned as dead for twenty-nine years; and afterwards attach to it such weight, and such weight only, as under all the circumstances you think it entitled to.

The expert evidence before you as to whether

defendant is suffering from hereditary or acquired disease, a disease incurred or contracted in childhood or one received in manhood, is of course important, and I trust it will aid you, but it is to be considered and passed upon by you in the light of your common sense and experience in life.

Evidence has been given showing the state of defendant's mind before or afterwards and at the time of the application for pension by defendant was made.

If the defendant at that time was an idiot, a a lunatic, or affected with insanity, he should be acquitted. The law, however, does not require the highest, or even a very large measure of intelligence, in order to hold one to responsibility. If at the time the defendant had sufficient mind to know right from wrong with reference to the particular transaction, then he was responsible. But if not, then he was incapable of committing crime.

In passing upon this question, reference should be had to defendant's conduct and conversation before and about the time and after he applied for a pension. In considering the question as to whether defendant is William Newby you may well inquire whether he is Daniel Benton, and for that purpose have reference to the description of, and recognition of, the various witnesses —witnesses recognizing him as Benton, as well as any resemblance you may have discovered between the son of Benton, according to the testimony of his mother, and defendant.

But, gentlemen, I forbear a general discussion of this evidence. In this country evidences go directly from the witnesses to the jury. The court's duty is performed when aid is attempted to be rendered in assisting the jury in applying or placing value upon certain of its phases, which, by reason of want of familiarity with rules in regard to evidence you are not able to render and satisfactorily dispose of.

It is scarcely necessary to say, yet it is a rule of law for benefit of defendant, the evidence, in your opinion, must establish his guilt beyond a reasonable doubt. This is an old and wise rule. The doubt, however, must be a reasonable one, arising out of the unsatisfactory character of the government's evidence. A reasonable doubt is not a mere possibility of defendant's innocence; it is more than this—it is an unsatisfied condition of the mind because of the unsatisfaction of the evidence to convict of the truth of the fact aforesaid. It is not demonstrating the truth of such fact ordinarily. The truth as to questions of fact is not demonstrative. If the evidence satisfies you of defendant's guilt to the same extent it would in your own minds authorize you to have with reference to the grave affairs of life, in a matter of importance to you, then you are satisfied beyond a reasonable doubt; or, to put it differently, if from the entire evidence you have an abiding conviction of the truth of the charge, then you should find defendant guilty; otherwise, you should acquit him. Your verdict is simply guilty or not guilty. You have nothing whatever to do with the punishment.

WIL

HIS COMRADES OF THE FORT!

TAKEN AT SPRI

1 Sod Upton.
2 C. H. White.
3 Hanson Goodrich.
4 James J. Watson.
5 S. M. Wallace.
6 David Holmes.
7 Newton McRill.
8 Samuel Bull.

NEWBY.

LLINOIS INFANTRY VOLUNTEERS.

D, ILL., JULY 15, 1893.

9 Thos. H. Harris.
10 Geo. A. Miller.
11 William Coburn.
12 Whalen Newby.
13 John Nell.
14 James Colbert.
15 William McNeely.

CHAPTER XI.

COMMENTS ON THE INSTRUCTIONS OF THE COURT.

THE case was tried by Hon. J. W. Allen, Judge of the United States Court for the Southern District of Illinois, who was appointed by President Cleveland during his first term. He is an able jurist and an accomplished gentleman. The legal portion of his life prior to his appointment has been spent in Southern Illinois. His home is at Cairo, we believe.

In our comments upon the instructions of this Court the reader is asked to consider that in the mind of the Court whatever of prejudice or bias that may have once existed has been removed, and to consider, each for himself, the question as to whether a man, by reason of his qualifications for positions of honor among men, may not so entirely get away from his former environments as to deal fairly with his fellow men in all things. The writer believes a man may do this, and the apparent "leaning" that seems to run through the instructions of the Court may raise the question as to why the special attention of the jury was called so forcibly to certain points, very accurately noted, the effect of which would naturally tend to fix their minds upon phases of the evidence in such a manner as to cause them to overlook other phases of evidence, the effect of which would be to establish a doubt of his guilt.

While a jurist is not supposed to take advantage of his superior knowledge of human nature, gathered from long experience and opportunity above that of almost everyone called as a juror, yet we must judge him in giving his instructions in this case, though so uncommon as not likely to occur again in a lifetime for importance, in the light of custom long established in criminal trials. We are to remember that the law puts a man upon trial charged by indictment with crime as nevertheless innocent until proven guilty, insomuch does it even try to teach us to look upon the person charged, but who comes clear, as having the same purity of character as though he had never been charged with crime. While this has long been attempted to be inculcated in the minds of men, nevertheless it leaves a little stain because of the record that even time does not efface, and sometimes the third and fourth generations are required to meet that record. If, perchance, he might have escaped trial on the charge from a technicality raised by astute council, or a defect in the indictment, or by reason of the many ways devised by practice to avoid the effects of actual transgression, and if a jury say "not guilty," the accused go acquit, the people have no appeal. Hence we may see the custom of the Court, in criminal cases, to lean a little to the people may be well founded, and not always the effect of bias or prejudice, and is exercised according to custom long found necessary for the protection of society. Yet in this case, after careful consideration of the instructions, we think His Honor may not have been warranted in saying to that jury as to how any class of witnesses reached their conclusions as to the facts to which they testify, and more especially in the face of the fact that they were not permitted by the Court to detail to the jury any of the facts or circumstances by which they reached their conclusions, whereby they were enabled to identify the claimant—the material question in the inquiry; His Honor further telling the jury that such testimony is often unreliable, thus taking from the jury the right to judge for themselves of its reliability,—their opportunity being equal to that of the Court in their judgment of how the witnesses arrived at their conclusion. The doctrine has never received legal sanction that any court should assist a jury by reference to its own experience, for the obvious reason that the experience of a jurist would have more weight than the evidence of many witnesses.

Then, again, reference is made by the Court to the jury that it may occur to them as remarkable that there is an entire absence of evidence offered as to when the claimant was taken to Andersonville, and how he got there, or the class of prisoners to which he belonged. By this reference a new point or question is raised in the mind of the jury not thought necessary in the trial of the case by either side. The trial being over, the suggestion coming from the Court may have had much influence, and the accused can only await the verdict.

The Court also tells the jury that it is important whether the disease with which claimant was suffering was hereditary or acquired; whether received in childhood or maturity. Tells them they may consider the expert testimony, but admonishes them to do so in the light of their common sense and their experience in life. This last suggestion is capable of at least two constructions. First, the jury may conclude from it that but little attention should be given to such evidence; or, second, that without it they may determine the cause of injuries that claimant received in the light of their own experience and common sense, unaided by such expert testimony. And judging from the verdict in this important case, the instructions of the Court received as much, or more, consideration than the evidence of the almost two hundred witnesses offered before them, from the fact that the time consumed by the jury from the moment of their retirement from the court-room until the return of their verdict into court was less than twenty minutes. The jury in this case was composed of the following named gentlemen:

John R. Thompson, Vermillion County.
John Easton, Athens "
Joseph Rogers, McLain "
Alex. Howard, Morgan "
G. W. Winchester, Champaign "
J. W. Hartwell, Williamson "
C. W. Hammond, Clark "

George Brown,	Piatt	County.
J. O. Krintor,	Schyler	"
John Lowry,	Sangamon	"
B. S. Graves,	"	"
John Kenny,	"	"

All questioned and qualified as in other cases. The most remarkable feature of this jury in their hearing of this case was the conduct of some of them from the beginning. They seemed to be wholly forgetful of their duty, notwithstanding the every-day admonitions of the Court that they must not speak of the case, not even among themselves, when, in fact, the conduct of some of them became so notorious that the Court, several days before the trial closed, found it necessary to place them in the hands of an officer. The verdict of the jury, coming in with such indecent haste, to say that it was not a surprise to the multitude present, the entire city, and the whole country, who had caught the interest from the wires during the trial, would be untrue. Surprise is a mild term—even violence seemed imminent on receipt of the verdict by the disappointed and surprised people.

Many able lawyers have found, in their practice in the higher courts of the government, that a difference seems to exist in the minds of the people. When a citizen is arrested upon the charge of crime against the government of the United States they seem to be overawed, as it were. The machinery is more powerful. While it moves slowly, yet it is with an irresistible force. It appears to the citizen that he is to receive justice without mercy—that the object is to make an example out of every man who gets into the clutches of its law. When a citizen is suspected of crime, detectives of long experience are put upon his track, who industriously follow it, and whose success often measures the time of his employment. They gather their evidence before they make the arrest—all that can be unearthed outside—then they interview the man, and what they can not "force-pump" out of him by their astute methods they even sometimes find it necessary themselves to go upon the stand and uncover all they consider necessary to give light on the case.

Then they get much free advertising by being interviewed, and giving their wonderful discoveries, which are spread before the public. Even in this case the wonderful exploits of McBride, the special government agent, were fully set forth in a long article in the Cincinnati *Enquirer*, a paper of great circulation, which showed clearly that the claimant was guilty, and this even before the return of the indictment against him, and the publication of this article, and the comments upon it by the local press, so fixed public opinion in the minds of the people against the claimant that it required much evidence to remove it. The claimant, being poor in purse and weak in mind, was put upon his trial in this condition, and required to proceed. The prosecution opened the case with a cloud of witnesses who had been discovered by McBride, brought from a foreign state by the government, and furnished with mileage, bed, and board, and prepared to substantiate almost every word of the statements of the interview heretofore referred to. Thus the prosecution of the case is closed by a full substantiation to the jury of almost every word previously published to the world, and read by the jury.

Up to this time the jury had been unrestrained (running at large). Newby or Benton, was the word at every store, shop, or boarding-house in the city. Then the opinion was Benton at the close of the prosecution. At this stage of the trial the jury were taken charge of by an officer, with the special duty enjoined upon him not to allow them to be approached by any person from the outside world—a circumstance probably suggested to the court by the condition of the public mind and the conduct of some of the jurymen with reference to it. So, in this condition the coming of the one hundred and sixty for the claimant of his neighbors, friends, and comrades of the old 40th Illinois, their evidence could not reach them, with the force added, of an immediate change in public pulse, after hearing their testimony. Hence, the effect of the change did not reach that jury, and the trial might have ceased at the close of the prosecution. Then the old aphorism, "that if you have a good case, try it by the court; if a bad one, let a jury come," is full of meaning, and warning as well; and what a menace to our jury system. The hearing of a case by the court is within his province, and because of his profession. Not so with juries; one professional on a jury renders the result uncertain.

The evidence in this case the reader has doubtless read with much care, and he may consider it in the light of the evidence of the witnesses as they have given it; together with all the light he may get from all the circumstances related in this book, many of which are as correct as much of the evidence produced at the hearing, to which and altogether, you may add your own experience with men and things ; and judge in the light of your common sense; and make up your verdict, which you may give ; not different from that jury ; but more time will be required in the consideration, and when done you may have a "reasonable doubt."

CAPT. J. W. HILL, FRIEND OF CLAIMANT.

CHAPTER XII.
CONCLUSION.

WHEN an old soldier writes a biography of another old soldier he may reasonably hope to find among the old veterans of the war an appreciative audience and his most charitable critics.

Many of us were in our small twenties and at school when the roar of the first guns from Fort Sumter reverberated through the land, firing the heart of the North, and "turning striplings into men, and peaceful citizens into veteran soldiers."

In those stirring times no class sprang forward with greater alacrity than the young men of the schools and colleges of the land. The halls of learning were deserted for the arduous duties of the camp; the text-book was exchanged for Hardee's Tactics; and the logic of the books for the more convincing logic of the cold steel.

When the war was over, we were too old, too crippled, and too poor to again enter the halls of learning, but we accepted the sacrifice with a good grace, and trudged homeward, delighted with the opportunity to show to an astonished world how an army of half a million of veteran American soldiers could in a day be transformed again into peaceful, law-abiding American citizens. So, with whatever stock of learning he had, each man fell to "hustling" for a livelihood in the ordinary vocations of life, and, although a good many years have passed, yet, by the mercy of God, we still live to enjoy the liberties of a free country, and by the forbearance of the "powers that be" we continue to receive our little pensions, which were intended to, and which in a measure do, compensate for the time, opportunities, and health lost during those years.

But, comrades, our ranks are fast thinning out. Time and disease have reduced brigades to the size of regiments; have reduced regiments to companies; and companies have dwindled to a corporal's guard, and often to a single man. Henceforth we must expect to pass away at a constantly accelerating rate.

When thirty years more have passed, the old veterans will be very few and very feeble. Like the old palsied sentinels that stand guard over the tomb of Napoleon Bonaparte, they will be the objects of melancholy interest and sympathy.

CONCLUSION.

Forty years hence, when the roll is called at the grand reunion where the silent majority have gathered beyond the grave, few will be absent, still lingering on the shores of time.

In that year, the year of our independence one hundred and fifty-seven, let the President of the United States send forth his proclamation calling together at the Capital all who responded to the call of Father Abraham, and served in the Great War of Freedom. Let every state send all that remains of her quota to Washington, that the Nation may gather there and do them reverence. How many will there be in all? One hundred? One score? Five? If there be only five, yea, if there be but one, let the chief executive, the cabinet, congress, and all the people, with uncovered heads, gaze upon him—the last man of that mighty human wall that stood between free institutions and the curse of slavery.

Comrades, we have seen some rough times, and our lives have been shortened somewhat by the destroying agencies incident to war, but we have lived a long time, and our lot has been a glorious one.

"Better fifty years in Europe than a cycle in Cathay."

Better ten years in free America than a hundred years in Europe.

Although we have shortened our lives by a few years in serving our country, we have lived more, seen more, enjoyed more of life in this time than if we had existed during the whole period of the Roman Empire.

Steam and electricity have annihilated time and distance, and have brought the whole world to our doors. There are no strangers, there are no foreigners now. To-day your little grandchildren may go with you to the World's Fair, and converse with the inhabitants from all around the globe, from sun-scorched Africa to the dwellers around the Pole. They may walk with you in the streets of Cairo, and buy trinkets from the king of the Cannibals.

We can lay our hands on the pulse of the world, and hear the murmur of the voice of the nations.

The era of wars seems to be passing away. Let us hope that we were actors in the last, as well as the greatest war of modern times. The principles of arbitration is likely henceforth to control, and questions which it once required the blood of thousands to settle will be settled with a drop of ink.

We live in a glorious age. Let us thank God that our lines have fallen to us in a pleasant place, and that ours has been the privilege of helping to perpetuate the principles of freedom that make our country glorious among the nations.

The stability of our government is founded upon the intelligence and patriotism of the common people, and is perfectly secure. The contentions of parties over the questions of tariff, finance, and fisheries are only questions of winter clothes, pocket money, and marketing, which come into the experience of every well-governed family.

Before laying down my pen I wish to express my honest conviction that every old soldier should see to it that the man who is the subject of this book should have a fair show, and receive the benefit of evenhanded justice.

The question of the prisoner's innocence should be settled beyond the peradventure of a doubt. Had a single slave been excluded from the benefits of Lincoln's proclamation, were it known to-day that a single negro was held in slavery by sanction of this government, the old soldiers and their children would rise up and demand his immediate and unconditional freedom. How much more then ought we to see that justice is done to one who voluntarily fought to save the country, and to set these men free. If this man be William Newby, he is not only " an unfortunate and much injured man," as stated by the Judge, but he is the subject of the most cruel injustice and the basest ingratitude ever shown by a civilized government to one of its subjects.

Think of it! You remember well the motives of patriotism that induced you to leave your home and enlist in the war. You remember the hardships and horrors of that service. Imagine yourself shot in the head and made a cripple in body and an imbecile in mind, wandering about over the country in whose service you were shot, seeking for food and shelter. Imagine yourself imprisoned for eleven long years in the capital of the state whose soil was wet with your blood. Suppose that after thirty years' wanderings you are picked up by your friends and sent to the War Department to receive the little paper so precious to every old soldier—your honorable discharge. You totter up to the door of the government and make known your request. A voice from within says: " You are a little tardy, old man; we turned off the 'discharge' clerk twenty-five years ago. We are out of the business, and have torn up all the blanks." You insist: "'This has been a long war to me; my story is a long one, and a sad one; but I am in no shape to tell it. You can get it from my folks, and the boys that were in the army with me. I can show you my wounds, my worn-out body, and my comrades can tell you when and where I fell. Ask my mates if I did not do my duty in your service. I am weary and well-nigh worn out, and only want that little paper and whatever pension the government is willing to bestow."

"The request is not regular" says the Department. "We will see about it."

They "see about it" with a vengeance.

An emissary is sent out to "see about it."

You are brought up before a judge who considers it his business to " see about it."

The jury steps out and for the fraction of eighteen minutes " sees about it."

The result is that you are torn from your home, the old blue coat is taken off your back, you are dressed in the garb of a convict, and put in the penitentiary for two years' hard labor.

This has been the history and this has been the fate of William Newby. It is an outrage too grievous to be borne, and every old soldier should make it his business to see that evenhanded justice is dealt out to this old man, who has been more unfortunate and more sinned against than were the victims of the Bastile or the Prisoner of Chillon.

NOTE BY THE AUTHOR.

I would be ungrateful, and my work would be incomplete, were I not to acknowledge the assistance received from others.

Mr. E. S. Robinson has aided me very materially in compiling and classifying the evidence at the trial.

Especial mention must be made of H. F. Sibley, Capt. N. S. McCowan, and J. Wagley Hill, the committee of assistance for the unfortunate man. The latter gentleman has been especially active in searching for the whereabouts of the "missing link," Dan Benton.

It is one of the novel features of this extraordinary case that the defense was not only required to prove the identity of the prisoner as Newby, but also to account for the fate of or produce the original Benton. The prosecution said, in effect: "We say this man is 'Rickety Dan' Benton. If you say it is Newby, then where is Dan Benton?" This conundrum being sprung when the defense had neither the time nor the money to investigate, had to remain for the time unanswered.

Since the trial, Mr. Hill has gone to work on the investigation with the energy worthy of a good cause, and with very gratifying results. It looks now as if the history or fate of Benton will be ferreted out. Think of the task of finding a boy who disappeared during the war. Think of the thousands of young men who leave their homes and never write to tell of their whereabouts. Think how unlikely Dan would be to write to a mother who was capable of returning him to the penitentiary for a reward of eighty-nine cents a year. Think of the thousands of graves all over the South marked "Unknown." Think of the thousands more that were never marked at all. Think of the number of bodies in the morgues of our cities stretched on slabs for identification, and of how many of them in the last thirty years have been buried in potters' fields. Think of the hundreds that have been run over by trains, or picked up as floaters in our rivers in the last thirty years. Think of Charley Ross. Think of the great number of advertisements in the daily papers offering large rewards for people who have disappeared from sight. Think that at this time one of the best known men in the West, a man high up in financial and social circles, has disappeared without apparent reason, and the best detective force in the world has failed to disclose his whereabouts. Think of all these things, and then the labors and success of Mr. Hill will be appreciated.

COL. S. G. HICKS, OF THE 40TH ILLINOIS.

APPENDIX.

A BRIEF ACCOUNT OF THE ORGANIZATION OF THE 40TH ILLINOIS INFANTRY UP TO THE BATTLE OF SHILOH, AND OF THE PART TAKEN IN THAT ENGAGEMENT.

(Compiled from History of 40th Illinois Infantry by Sergeant E. J. Hart.)

ABOUT the first day of May, 1861, Stephen G. Hicks, a lawyer of Salem, Marion County, Illinois, commenced laboring for the purpose of raising a body of men for the military service of the United States. The public mind had become very much excited in consequence of the seeming near approach of the outburst of rebellion; and all were ready to rush to arms to rescue our loved government from dissolution and ruin. The persevering and determined Hicks, by his masterly eloquence and earnest appeals in behalf of our once happy country, experienced no difficulty in procuring a sufficient number of men to form a complete regiment.

But many were so impatient for the order, Forward march! that they abandoned the one they had chosen first for leader, and attached themselves to other regiments which had been already accepted and were then on their way to take the field. In this manner several companies which he had been instrumental in organizing, and which he hoped to be able to form into his proposed regiment, were taken from him. Determined not to be baffled in his intentions to lead a regiment of men into the field, he immediately commenced a rigid canvassing through the surrounding country. He addressed large and enthusiastic assemblies on the subject of the distracted condition of our country and the importance of prompt and immediate action of all truly loyal citizens for her salvation. Such meetings were held by him in the counties of Clay, Wayne, Franklin, Hamilton, Marion, and White, and by them succeeded in organizing companies and personally endeavored to have them properly officered by good, reliable, and efficient men, as it was his intention to take the best men into the service that Illinois had yet sent, and which he intended making the Egyptian regiment. About the last of May the required number of men was reported to him ready to meet his orders to rendezvous at any time.

He immediately informed Governor Yates that he had a regiment of men ready to enter the service, and wished to be received at once. Governor Yates soon replied that he had already furnished the Secretary of War the full quota of troops from his state, and that under no consideration could he accept any more. Hicks then then addressed a letter to the Secretary of War, Hon. Simon Cameron, begging him to receive his regiment at once, stating that he had as good a body of men as was ever taken into the service, which he very much desired to lead against the rebellious foe. Cameron soon replied that it was impossible for him to admit any more troops from Illinois, as he had already accepted more than her quota. Hicks resolved to hold his men in readiness, feeling assured that the executive authorities were underrating the strength of the rebellion, and that the government would soon need more troops to effectually crush out the gigantic monster of treason and infamy, and that he would stand at the head of the lists of applicants and thereby secure an early admission. His subordinate officers, impatient to be off, visited him continually at his residence to see if there was any possible chance for them to be allowed to enter the field; but he advised them to keep their men in readiness, be patient, and that in course of time they would undoubtedly have an opportunity of engaging in the work they seemed to desire so much.

On the 22d of July, 1861, our army, under command of General McDowell, met with a disastrous defeat at Bull Run.

On the 24th of July Hicks telegraphed to the Secretary of War that he still had his regiment in perfect readiness for the service, and wished to be admitted immediately. And on the 25th of July the Secretary accepted his regiment, and telegraphed him to report to Governor Yates for further instructions. Thus the 40th was accepted by the Secretary of War in advance of the call by Congress for four hundred thousand troops, and were to take the field as soon as the executive authorities made the proposed call at law. Accordingly Hicks visited the governor at Springfield and reported his acceptance, and also made all necessary preparations for camping, etc.

He received orders to go into camp at Clear Lake, near Springfield, on the 6th of August. He then went to St. Louis and engaged transportation of the president of the Ohio & Mississippi Railroad for his regiment to Sandoval, when he returned to his residence and issued orders to the respective company commanders to rendezvous their companies at Sandoval on the morning of the 5th of August.

Sunday morning, the 4th, the Fairfield company, Capt. Hooper, the Mount Erie and Jeffersonville company, Capt. Ulm, and the Burnt Prairie company, Capt. E. Stuarts, all met at Ensley's Point, on Indian Prairie. In the afternoon the New Baltimore company, Capt. Scott, joined us on our way to the road, which made four companies in our procession, that were marching to Flora, where we arrived about five o'clock in the evening.

As we boarded the cars the next morning we witnessed the most exciting scene ever beheld in our lives. Language fails to describe the excitement of that particular moment. Hundreds of parents, brothers, sisters, and friends mingled their voices in the tremendous shouts for the Union, as their loved ones were starting from their happy homes to meet the traitors to our country. Aged fathers with streaming eyes cheered their sons as they were just entering on their toilsome and perilous duties. Five companies were then with us; the four companies which embarked at Flora, with the Clay City company, Capt. More, which took the cars at Clay City. After a few miles' run we came to Xenia, where the Mount Carmel and Xenia company, Capt. Hoskinson, was waiting to join us.

The cars now moved on to Salem, a distance of eighteen miles; when we reached that place the Hamilton County company, Capt. Hall, with a part of the Salem and Vandalia company, Capt. S. Stuart, were in waiting for us, and soon were on the train, when in the usual manner we again started on amidst the united shouts of many and ardent friends, and passed on to the village which was our place of rendezvous.

At Salem our new colonel, S. G. Hicks, whom everyone regarded as the father of our new regiment, took the cars, and with his old, rusty Mexican saber in hand, passed through the entire train, which produced quite a sensation on all those present. We arrived at Sandoval about ten o'clock a. m., where we met the Kinmundy company, Capt. Both, and a part of the Salem and Vandalia company.

At two o'clock in the evening all the companies were ordered to muster, and to form the regiment in close columns of companies in front of the American House, which they did at the appointed hour. Stephen G. Hicks now presented himself at the head of the column, and addressed them in the following manner:

"Gentlemen: I am happy to see you assembled together to-day, and in such a favorable condition. I have labored among you earnestly for the purpose of organizing a regiment of men for the United States service, and through my labors and your own perfect knowledge of the great principles of right and justice I have been able to obtain my much desired object. You have nobly done your first and highest duty to your country in thus so promptly turning out and rushing to her assistance in this her darkest hour of peril. As I have often told you before, in public addresses, it is my intention to go with you, and with you share the toils and tribulations of a soldier's life, and with you I am ready to meet the bloody crew on the bloody field of conflict who have dared to insult our national standard and to deny her sovereignty. I know you are all men of veracity and true courage, and the best Egyptian Illinois affords, and I do earnestly desire to have the great honor of leading such a band of noble men into the field; yet I do not feel disposed to take such a high and responsible position without the united wishes of every one of you. I will now pledge you my sacred honor as a man that if you see proper to choose me for your colonel, I will be with you to the end. I will ever be to you as a father. I will labor assiduously for your welfare while in camp, and in every condition in which you may be placed it will be the delight of my heart to render each and every one of you any aid or comfort which lies in my power. And when we are called to fight our enemies I will lead the way. I will be in your front on the advance, and on the retreat I will guard your rear. We will advance against the foe as a united band of brothers fighting in the same great and righteous cause."

Cheer after cheer rent the air as the illustrious and patriotic man spoke to his attentive audience. After speaking in this manner for some time, while the most intense interest and wildest excitement prevailed, he said, " Now, gentlemen, if there is any man here, or among you, wishes to ask for your votes for colonel he is at perfect liberty to come forward." Here he ceased speaking to wait for any who might wish to offer for the position, but no one coming out a profound silence reigned until he proceeded by saying, "All that wish me for their commanding officer will please make known that desire by raising your right hands." In an instant all hands were lifted into the air at arm's length. Next was a scene of mingled enthusiasm and commotion which baffles all description. Peal after peal of most tremendous shouts of approbation and excitement and satisfaction was indulged in by everyone. The newly made colonel now retired, while each company broke ranks and spent the day as they wished.

Thus, through the untiring energies of our much-loved colonel, the 40th Regiment was at last organized, and one of the best men the country afforded placed at its head without a dissenting voice. The Colonel had his men so completely in readiness for marching that, notwithstanding they were scattered over seven different counties, and were busily engaged in their usual vocations of life, sixty hours after he had issued orders at his residence in Salem to the various companies to meet at Sandoval, every man was there according to orders. Another important fact was that the regiment did not cost the government one cent until it took the cars for its place of rendezvous, as the Colonel had defrayed all expenses up to that time.

In the evening we started for Camp Butler, and Col. Hicks thus met his engagement to go into camp on the 6th day of August.

The regiment was sworn into the service the 10th day of August and on the 11th started to Jefferson Barracks, where we arrived the same day at twelve o'clock.

On the morning of the 31st of August, at early dawn, we took a steamer and moved down the great Mississippi River.

On Sunday, September 1, at nine a. m., we arrived at Bird's Point, Mo., which is opposite Cairo, Illinois.

On Thursday, September 5, 1861, we drew our military uniform, and on Saturday, September 7, we received orders to move to Paducah, Ky., where our regiment remained for six months.

There was great dissatisfaction on the part of the regiment on account of their prolonged stay at Paducah, and of not being permitted to take part in the capture of Forts Henry and Donaldson. However, on Thursday, March 6, the long-desired orders came to march, and embarking on the steamers Sallie List and Golden Gate we started for the Tennessee River, Colonel Hicks being in command of the night brigade, and the regiment commanded by Colonel Boothe.

On Friday, March 7, we passed Fort Henry. On the 8th we reached Savannah. After remaining several days on the transport boats, varied with a little fatigue duty on shore, on Monday,

March 17, at one o'clock a. m., we were ordered to go ashore, with two days' rations

The 6th Iowa Infantry was there attached to our brigade, and their commander, Col. John Adair McDowell, being Col. Hicks' senior, took command of the brigade. After a scanty morning meal, prepared under unfavorable circumstances, we marched out at eight o'clock. We moved about four miles from the landing, and halted in an old field, where we remained over the night, sending out pickets, who were stationed at a log meeting house belonging to the Methodist denomination, since so notable as the Shiloh Church, from which the great battle fought in that vicinity derived its name.

Thus the 40th boys were the first Union soldiers that stood picket at the Shiloh Church.

Thursday, March 20, our camp equipage and all our baggage had at last reached us. Our tents were soon put up, and our camp permanently located near Owl Creek, on the Rolla Road, where we remained encamped during our stay at that post. Our brigade was camped on the extreme right of the army, and the other regiments and batteries of the great army of the Tennessee were posted between us and the landing.

Sunday, March 30, was a beautiful morning.

There seemed to be more than ordinary quiet through the camp of the 40th, as though the day of rest was at that time to be observed with due reverence. Many of the boys were thoughtfully perusing books or papers, and some, I am happy to say, reading good books; while others were busy writing letters to friends, or reviewing some kind missive which had been received—all causing the camp to wear a sober and meditative air seldom ever noticed before. Under these favorable circumstances Chaplain Massey resolved to hold divine service at the hour of eleven o'clock a. m. His remarks were affecting, showing the uncertainty of life, and consequently the importance of ever being ready for death, the certain lot of all. He stated that, in consideration of the uncertainties of war, it was hard to tell what a day would bring forth, and that ere another Christian Sabbath would pass many of the number then present might be in vast eternity. However lightly anyone might have reflected on that solemn yet truthful thought at that time, there was no doubt, after the horror of the eventful Sabbath day following, in which so many of our loved comrades were laid low by the hands of our enemies, that their minds were impressed by the importance of giving that solemn reflection due consideration.

BATTLE OF SHILOH.

On the evening of Friday, the 4th of April, there was a smart skirmish to the south of our camp, two or three miles distant. The reports of fire-arms were plainly heard, which caused some suspicion that there were enemies not far distant, and some precautionary arrangements were made in the regiment. When firing commenced, the long roll was beaten in our regiment, and we stacked arms on the color line ready for action should it be necessary. In the evening Company B, under command of Lieut. Harrelson, was sent out to strengthen the picket line in our front, which was about one half mile beyond Owl Creek.

Saturday, 5th. That morning Company E, under command of Capt. Ulm, was ordered and stationed a short distance in the rear of the picket line to serve as its support in case of an attack by the enemy. Quiet continued during the day, and many of the boys began to doubt the probability of the rebels troubling us. During the night, however, Company B's boys, who were on the front line, were convinced that an enemy was hovering near, as they could hear them moving continuously through the brush.

Sunday, April 6. As soon as daylight came all doubts about the enemy being near our lines were dispelled, for their movements could be plainly observed through the woods. About sunrise an occasional shot could be heard on our left; and in a few moments the attacking rebel column made its appearance, and Company E, the support, was ordered on the line, which command was readily obeyed, the company going to the edge of an open field on the line, and, lying down, remained there a few moments when it fired a volley across the field. This was a signal for our pickets to rally. The rebels' line of skirmishers then stole up and fired on the pickets. One ball took effect, killing a man belonging to Company E instantly, being the first man of the 40th who lost his life in action. The pickets then began to fall back slowly, firing as they retired.

The rebels planted one piece of artillery, which fired three times as a signal for their entire line to move forward. They continued to press our line, which was drawn in slowly, until it reached the camp of our regiment, when the two picket companies took their respective positions on the line which was drawn up in front of our quarters, with the 46th Ohio Volunteer Infantry and the

6th Iowa Infantry on our right. The regiment was soon ordered to move, which it did, passing over the ravine in our front, and taking a position on the opposite hill. There we remained for some time, while there was some hard fighting close on our left, from which we could discern our men giving back, and occasionally a ball would whizz past us, striking a tree or something else. A column of infantry was then seen moving down the opposite slope of Owl Creek, in blue uniform, which was really the enemy, but they deceived us. The officers declared they were our men until they were close on us, in as good position as they desired, without any resistance. We then fired a volley at them, when the Colonel ordered "By the right of companies to the rear into column." We were to fall back to the Rolla Road, which we did, marching by the right flank, arriving on the road, and forming into line. There considerable confusion occurred, as all the teams, and as much valuable property as could be loaded easily on the wagons, were driving for the rear as rapidly as possible. The troops on our left were pressed very hard, and were still retreating slowly, fighting with great desperation. This made it unsafe, and perfectly useless for us, occupying the right, to remain there longer, and we were compelled to abandon our camp and retreat. We followed the Rolla Road toward the river, marching column, with left in front, until we passed our brigade headquarters, when we marched by the flank toward the north, through a dense thicket. The rebels were closely in pursuit, and would send an occasional ball rather nearer us than was agreeable. Giving back in that manner so long, with the enemy hotly pursuing us, without receiving any resistance, was encouraging them to follow, and greatly confusing the men of our regiment, who were willing and anxious to contend for every inch of ground over which we were retreating. We were soon halted and thrown into line of battle, fronting to the east, and extending along the brow of a bank, behind which was a large swamp, and on which there had once been a fence, causing a thick undergrowth of sassafras. We then, as rapidly as possible, got our position, and laid down to await the advance of the enemy, who soon showed themselves on the next hill, directly east of us, only a short distance off. Their banner could be distinctly seen when they opened on us, making the brush rattle around us. We then poured a heavy fire into their ranks, when they replied by firing several charges of canister shot from a fieldpiece, doing us great damage, wounding several, and some mortally. Another well-directed volley from our good muskets drove the rebels from their ground, which was fortunate for us, as in that position they separated us entirely from the other part of the army, which might have resulted in our capture. Seeing this opportunity to extricate ourselves from that precarious position, we immediately advanced across the valley and to the ground just abandoned by the rebels, marching in line, leaving our wounded to be taken to an old building close by used as a hospital. When the point just spoken of was reached we marched by the left flank in a northerly direction for about one quarter of a mile, then bearing to the east for a short distance we halted in a field near some old buildings, when we marched in line of battle across the fences into an open wood, nearly two hundred yards distant, and rested in a ravine, on a spring branch, for some time. While in that position we were shielded from the artillery fire of the enemy. About that time there was a desperate fight between one of our batteries and the rebels, the shots passing continually over our heads, doing us no injury, however, only causing us to hover near earth in earnest.

About eleven o'clock we were ordered forward to relieve a regiment in our front, which was pressed, and was falling back. We moved in line of battle up the hill about fifty yards, when we came into a narrow open space, in plain view of the enemy. There the regiment we were to relieve were firing rapidly, and when they saw us they cheered loudly, waving their hands and welcoming us to their relief. We passed them about thirty yards and began firing, which we kept up with great spirit and determination for a considerable length of time, during which there was a complete shower of grape, canister, and musket-shot mowing down our gallant boys with great slaughter. It was in that place we lost so many of our brave men while, without flinching, they defiantly held their ground. There was great diversity of opinion relative to the length of time we were in that hard struggle, but those best qualified to know say that it did not exceed an hour and a half, during which we lost forty-six enlisted men killed, and a great number in wounded. Col. Hicks, in the thickest of the fight, was in the front, urging his men on, directing their fire into a rebel battery close in our front, from which we succeeded in driving its gunners, when his horse was shot from under him. As soon as the Colonel recovered his feet again, a bullet struck him in the left shoulder, rendering him almost helpless. His orderly, with the help of others, conveyed him back to the river, that he might receive surgical aid. The regiment was ordered to retreat, which it did, marching back over the same ground on which it had advanced.

After retreating some distance, Major Smith ordered a halt, and, after considerable difficulty, succeeded in getting our thinned ranks in order again, when we laid down for rest and protection from the enemy's shells. Soon some General's Aid passed by, inquiring, "What regiment is that?" To which the Major responded, "The 40th Illinois." The Aid then said, "In the name of God, why are you not moving against the enemy?" The Major responded, "We have expended all our cartridges." The Aid replied, "Then fix bayonets, and you can meet them when they come; for they are massing their forces in our front, and will evidently press us with great strength and renewed vigor." The Major then formed the regiment in line ready for an emergency.

At four o'clock we were ordered back toward the river to support the line of heavy siege guns, which had been formed there. There the regiment spent the night, without any refreshments and but little repose, remaining in line and under arms all night. Early next morning we were furnished with an abundant supply of rations, which was welcomely received and speedily devoured, as by that time we could relish army rations.

Our orders were that we were to be under command of Gen. Nelson, of Buell's army, which was then participating in the fight and to operate as his reserve. Gen. Nelson's command was on the left, and soon engaged the enemy with his advance, our regiment following in the rear as the reserve. The enemy's balls would fly past us continually, but seldom ever injuring anyone. Our troops were driving the rebels slowly and steadily, and our boys following them within supporting distance. The left of the front line being pressed, our regiment and one battery were ordered there. We marched by the left flank along the line until we gained our position on the left, where there was some rapid firing done, wounding some of our boys and killing one. By the assistance of the artillery we soon succeeded in completely routing the enemy and driving them from the ground from which they had been twice driven before. The enemy was then in full retreat, and our boys, notwithstanding they were greatly fatigued, seemed eager to follow them up, giving them their parting compliments with leaden messengers. The enemy's skirmishers continued to fire at us from behind some tents, trees, etc., in our front, until we were ordered to fix bayonets, move forward, and find out their strength. Accordingly we passed the tents, the enemy falling back. Their fire slackening, we halted, and remained there until evening.

About sundown we moved back one half mile, stopping on a road which was very muddy, where we were posted on picket guard. During the night a heavy rain fell, causing our situation to be exceedingly disagreeable, as all were compelled to stand on post in the rain without any shelter. The boys still say that the Monday night of the Shiloh battle was the most disagreeable night they ever spent in the army.

Tuesday, 8th. In the morning we moved to the camps of the 71st O. V. I., where we helped ourselves to some grub which we found there. We were ordered to remain there and bury the dead that were near that place. While there the regiment in whose camps we were stationed came in and complained of our taking possession, when our boys told them they had driven the rebel; from there, and being much in need of rations thought they had a right to help themselves. Major Smith being sick during the day, Capt. Hall was in command of the regiment. After having labored all day in burying the dead we rested for the night on the same ground we had occupied.

Wednesday, 9th. That morning Gen. Sherman sent orders to Maj. Smith to return to the regiment's old quarters, which we did at once. We soon reached, greatly wearied, our quarters, glad of the opportunity of resting once more. Many of our little affairs about camp had been destroyed by the enemy. Our knapsacks were all robbed of clothing or little friendly mementoes, such as miniatures of loved ones, which the villains generally threw on the ground and stamped on them. The remaining part of our stay in that camp was the most unpleasant we ever spent in camp, for there was no joyousness or life in the camp; all seemed to mourn some sad calamity, and besides mental depression there was a general prostration of the physical powers, all appearing languid, dull, and sluggish. We all remember, with feelings of sadness, what a distressing solemnity prevailed throughout the 40th, and it seemed as if the regiment could never recover from the shock. Sickness soon followed, making things still worse. All our boys who were wounded were either sent to their homes or hospitals.

Col. S. Hicks, immediately after he received his wound, was removed to the landing and placed on a large hospital boat, which started down the river on the evening of Tuesday, April 7, and arrived at Mound City on the evening of Friday, 10th. He was immediately taken to a hospital, where, by kind nurses and competent and experienced surgeons, he was attentively cared for. After remaining there until the 18th of April, he was taken to his home at Salem, Ill., where he suffered very severely from disease and the effect of his wound. As soon as his health would permit, he returned to his regiment, which he joined at Lafayette on the 18th of July, 1862.

www.ingramcontent.com/pod-product-compliance
Lightning Source LLC
Chambersburg PA
CBHW030811230426
43667CB00008B/1162